P. 5-6 missing.

HARLEY EARL AND THE DREAM MACHINE

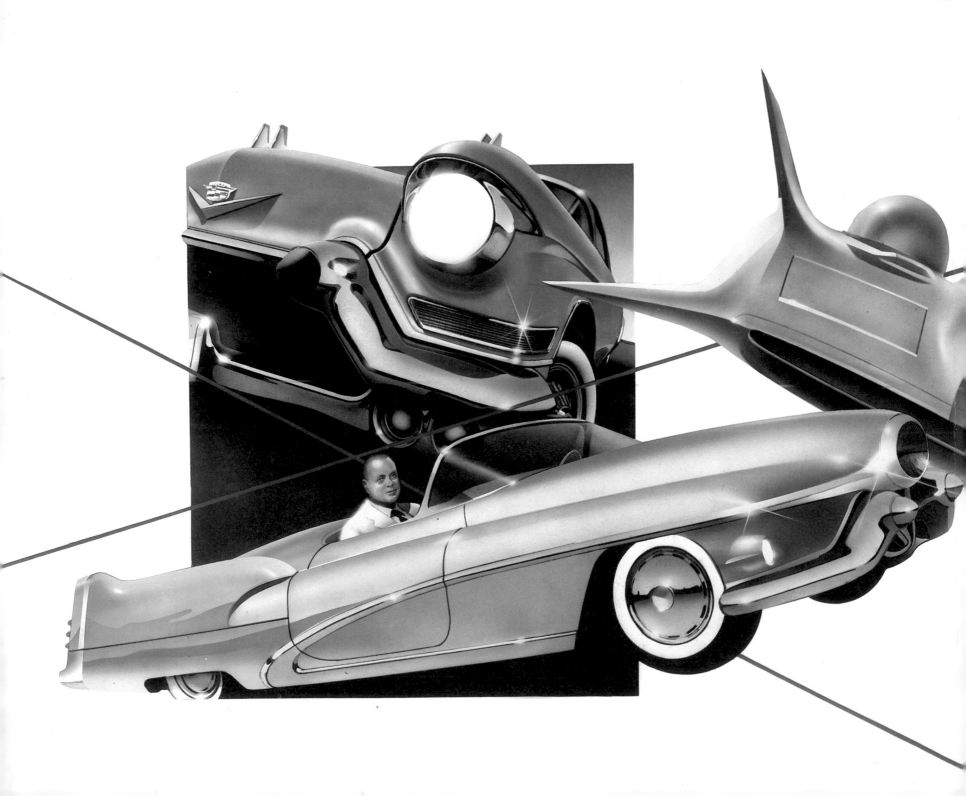

HARLEY EARL
AND THE DREAM MACHINE
STEPHEN BAYLEY

WITH FIVE PLATES BY PHILIP CASTLE

ALFRED A. KNOPF · NEW YORK · 1983

PAGE I 1953 Chevrolet Corvette.

FRONTISPIECE Harley Earl at the wheel of the Le Sabre dream car, with the Firebird III and a detail of the 1954 Cadillac.
Painting by Philip Castle.

PAGE 6 The Cadillac Aerocar (above), for the 1933 Chicago World's Fair, and the celebrated Buick 'Y' Job (below) were not the first but were the most thorough exercises in informal styling which Harley Earl gave to General Motors before the Second World War.
Painting by Philip Castle.

PAGE 7 The tail fin, or fishtail fender, was the most successful and egregious of styling motifs which Harley Earl introduced in his thirty-two years of running design at General Motors. An inspired piece of symbolism, it was derived from Earl's romance with the air, in particular with the astonishing Lockheed P38. The twin tail booms and rudders of the pursuit plane were translated into the vestigial tail fins of the 1948 Cadillac Sedanet (foreground), the car which inspired the British Bentley Continental.
Painting by Philip Castle.

Library of Congress Cataloging in Publication Data
Bayley, Stephen.
  Harley Earl and the dream machine.
  1. Earl, Harley. 2. Automobiles—United States—History. 3. Automobile engineers—United States—Biography. I. Title.
TL140.E23B39 1983   629.2'31'0924 [B]   83–48024
ISBN 0-394-53244-9

Manufactured in Italy   First American Edition

THIS IS A BORZOI BOOK
PUBLISHED BY ALFRED A. KNOPF, INC.

INTRODUCTION
DREAMING OUT LOUD

IT WAS THE BEST OF TIMES. It was America in the fifties and the sky was wide open and blue. Scarcity had disappeared off the map of human concerns. Indeed, the American consumer was so near satiety the manufacturers feared that the end result would be the unthinkable consequence that satisfied consumers would forget the itch of demand. So they set about to dissatisfy the consumer by bringing before him ever more novelty to excite his cupidity and, by extension, to keep the mechanism of wealth turning.

Cars were an essential part of this scheme, but they were not treated cynically. The beauty and the humanity of the idea was that you could not succeed in the automotive industry unless you gave the customer what he wanted, although the long lead times of mass production meant that the manufacturers and the designers they employed had to anticipate by about four years what citizens in St Paul, Anchorage and Tampa *actually* wanted to park in their drives.

It was an age of optimism: one commentator said of the fifties that in a world which allowed the American car to come into being, anything was possible. With less ambivalence, John Keats wrote in *The Insolent Chariots* that 'If Detroit is right . . . there is little wrong with the American car that is not wrong with the American public.' This is the poignancy of a passed moment which is now thirty years old. Woodrow Wilson called the American car a picture of 'the arrogance of wealth' and now it has gone. But for a moment it was unique: the plastic evidence of the most exhaustive and inventive probing of the consumer's id by any industry ever.

LEFT Harley Earl at his desk in the General Motors Building. As one contemporary said, he was like a Roman Emperor in Constantinople. Never in the history of Western industrial civilization has one man had such an authoritarian influence over a world of values.

PREVIOUS PAGES The
American sports car of the
fifties was a creation of
Harley Earl. The sculptural
forms, the associative details,
the colours and the names
were like a flushing-out of
the American psyche.
Clockwise from left: 1953

Chevrolet Corvette; 1954
Pontiac Bonneville show car;
1955 La Salle II (which
revised the first styling job
Earl had done for GM): 1954
Buick Wildcat; 1956 Pontiac
Club de Mer; 1956 Olds-
mobile Golden Rocket.
Painting by Philip Castle.

A lot of this probing and most of the inventiveness came from General Motors. Chief wizard in their den of kitsch was Harley Earl, whose years in charge of General Motors' styling section made him responsible for fifty million vehicles between 1927, when he joined the corporation from Hollywood, and 1959, when he retired to Palm Beach. Viewed in terms of numbers and of finance, Harley Earl was the most influential designer of the twentieth century.

People who knew him or worked for him during his Detroit years describe him as intimidating. If he smiled at you, something he did rarely, it made your day. If you heard him shouting at a colleague, you trembled in your colleague's place. One man said, 'He looked like he could kill you; a near miss would have done.' Earl was physically huge, a fact which discouraged any animated exchange of views between him and his employees. As a designer, he never lifted a pencil and he developed an atmosphere in his studios and workshops which they say was like Constantinople about fifteen hundred years ago. He would take meetings or listen to presentations sprawled in a high-style Mies van der Rohe Barcelona chair, suntanned, wearing a Florida summer suit, and he would point to offending details with a foot clad in hand-made English shoes.

He was so meticulous a dresser that, as a studio junior from the fifties recalled, his shoes looked as if they had trees inside them even when he was wearing them. He kept duplicate wardrobes stored in his ample office closet so that if the swampy atmosphere of a Michigan afternoon threatened to dampen at the creases his polychromatic linen suit, he could change before cocktails into an identical get-up. In just about everybody's estimation it was as if he was in permanent audition for 'The Most Unforgettable Man I Ever Met' series.

The staff was, of course, always deferential: they called him 'Misterearl' – all one word – and would not look up from their desks while he was in their studio. Harley Earl himself was, however, less confidently compact when it came to pronunciation. The word 'aluminium', which, things being what they were, he had to use fairly often, always raised a snigger among the juniors. 'I'd love to have a recording of him saying the word,' Dick Teague, now head of Styling at American Motors, recalled, because he managed to get into it at least two more syllables than the dictionary allowed.

Although he was a quiet man his stature allowed him to subdue whole rooms of people. He called those people who equivocated with world-improving and European good taste 'design eunuchs'. His opinions were not loosely held because once they had sedimented themselves into the primitive structure of his brain they were ineradicable. Nor were his opinions the products of long, meditative processes: they came hot off the griddle. Misterearl had charisma in spades.

He disdained his glasses and only wore them when he ate his habitual cheese sandwich at lunchtime. Those fifty million cars he designed without them.

General Motors under Harley Earl was the source of all the styling clichés in car design which we now take to have been inevitable: chrome, two-tone paint, tail fins, hardtops, wraparound windshields. . . . All these features, and some more esoteric ones besides, he invented for the corporation's vehicles of desire during the period when the executives realized that cars were more important than mere transport. Continuously, he made new diversions for an exhausted world. In 1956, the Chevrolet Division of General Motors scored a record market penetration of twenty-eight per cent. Its smartest product was the Bel Air, a four-door hardtop with a 270 hp engine to propel its coloured, chromed and textured cabin to speeds for which its brakes and its road holding were not adequate. Yet, if the medieval

Firebirds I, II and III were gas
turbine show cars whose
combination of pop science–
fiction nomenclature and
Roman numerology betrayed
a confused American taste
for technology mixed with
the sanction of a distant,
assumed tradition. The forms
and details of each car were
derived from the imagery of
the air, in particular from the
Douglas A4 Skyray which
succeeded the Lockheed P38
as a source of inspiration to
Earl. Clockwise from left:
Firebird I, 1954; Douglas A4
Skyray; Firebird III, 1958;
Firebird II, 1956 (foreground).
Painting by Philip Castle.

scholastics believed that the human soul might resemble a shrivelled raisin, the 1956 Chevrolet Bel Air was, according to the editors of *The Consumer's Guide*, the architecture of the American psyche made visible. By Harley Earl.

There was an element of social class in the cars and in the achievement. Earl came from California and spent his working life in Grosse Pointe, Michigan. He was unknown in New York and New England, where the Euro-centric design establishment lived. He was also separate from, although contemporary with, that first generation of American industrial designers, including Raymond Loewy and Norman Bel Geddes, who operated from Manhattan. You can see the cars as products of Midwestern gaudiness, made by the people who liked to serve beer instead of champagne at coming-out parties. In New England they were treated with disdain: America's second most influential designer, the Harvard educated Eliot Noyes of New Canaan, Connecticut, the man who designed the entire corporate face and product line of IBM, was driving Land-Rovers and Porsches while Earl and his men were designing the Cadillac Eldorado Seville Brougham hardtop and other cars with culturally confusing names. The difference was that while Eliot Noyes' work for IBM sought stasis in perfect clean forms, derived from European models and intended to appeal to corporate executives, Earl's work for General Motors had to appeal to blue-collar workers in Iowa.

These General Motors cars of Harley Earl were the symbols of a massive public fantasy to which most of the citizens of the United States subscribed and to which a large part of the rest of the world aspired. They were brought about by a deliberate corporate policy of encouraging dreams. Harley Earl invented the dream car at a moment in American history when the future seemed rosy rather than intimidating and when there was confidence that a better future would be brought about more quickly by ever increasing consumption of ever changing style. The dream car became a world famous symbol of the American public's growing and narcissistic fascination with the life it felt it could expect in the future.

The series of cars began in 1937 with a Buick 'Y' Job and continued through thirty-seven ever more bizarre conceptions, ending up in 1958 with the gas turbine Firebird III, a Flash Gordon vehicle with the passengers separated in their own bubbles, and the steering replaced by electromechanical bells and whistles, while pseudo-aerodynamic stabilizers were provided to fillet pedestrians. Still, as late as 1959, three years before Ralph Nader called the Chevrolet Corvair 'one of the greatest acts of industrial irresponsibility in the present century', General Motors' lyrical Public Relations department was able to call the crazy Firebird 'the auto industry's continual probing of better transportation tomorrows'.

Of course, that tomorrow never came. A US Secretary of Defense once said that what was good for General Motors was good for America. That quotation did not remain true for long, but while it did American cars were America's master product. This is a book about what was good for General Motors. And it did not last.

CARS FOR THE STARS

HARLEY EARL IN HOLLYWOOD

HARLEY EARL WAS BORN IN HOLLYWOOD on 22 November 1893, the son of J. W. Earl who since 1889 had been a local coachbuilder, making wagons, carriages and racing sulkies for the Mexican farmers and ranchers who preceded the movie industry as the denizens of the Los Angeles suburb. Hollywood, according to Ethel Barrymore, was entirely unreal, 'a glaring, gaudy, nightmarish set, built in the desert'. By Californian standards the Earl family was almost dynastically rooted: although Harley's father came from Michigan (where he had worked as a lumberjack and at a sawmill), his mother had been born there, the daughter of a civil dignitary. They were a well-established and prosperous unit and Earl senior was in a social position which allowed him to anticipate the potential of the private car. His awareness was given form in 1908 when he changed the name of his company to the Earl Automobile Works. Its business was making the exact kind of bolt-on accessories that Harley Earl was later to eradicate from the motor trade when he provided in the new mass-produced cars every option and appliance that could be dreamed of . . . and some that could not.

1911 was an apocalyptic year for the United States. It was then that the Horsley Brothers rented an abandoned and run-down tavern in Hollywood at Sunset and Gower, and used it to record film actors, most of them drunk, who performed screenplays for Edison's new moving picture machines. In the same year the Earl Automobile Works began to offer whole custom-made bodies for cars and trucks (as well as fuselages for the Glen L. Martin Company, one of the pioneers in Californian aerospace whose name became woven into the history of American

LEFT As a car designer in Hollywood, Harley Earl's commissions were custom-built bodies for the first generation of movie stars. This one, for Mary Miles Minter, is characteristically sculptural.

The Earl Automobile Works emerged from the coachbuilding shop established by Harley Earl's father. It was one of the pioneer industries of Los Angeles, providing custom-made components for cars during the era before the manufacturers began to cater to the individual consumer's needs. It was at this time that primeval decisions about the basic types of American car — such as sports *equals* open — were made and the imagery to support them began to emerge. LEFT Page from the Earl company's catalogue. BELOW AND OPPOSITE Renderings by Harley Earl for custom-built bodies by the Don Lee Corporation, which bought the Earl Automobile Works in 1919.

20

Harley Earl. *c.* 1903.

industry as did Harley Earl's).

Eventually the custom-made bodies began to supercede the accessories as the main part of the Earl company's business. With untaxed salaries to spend on whims and baubles, the first generation of film stars was beginning to demand special treatment for their newly acquired cars. As Raymond Chandler once said, 'Hollywood has all the personality of a paper cup'; just as the bland stuff of the cup required decoration and embellishment, so did the chassis of the actors. The company was already doing a brisk trade in chariots and Napoleonic funeral cars as props for the studios, but now it was the Earl Automobile Works' job to provide the stars with cars that were visibly different from the regular.

The first Earl creations, which were not completely new cars but highly modified standard models, marked a period of consolidation both for the city itself and for the young Harley Earl. He had been given an aegrotat from Stanford University after a track and field injury there had led to septicaemia, and he was now getting ready to take over from his father, whose own mind had been taken off the family business by the demands of his second marriage.

By about 1918 the first entire cars built by the Earl Automobile Works began to appear at the Los Angeles Auto Show. Harley Earl's name was seen in the papers for the first time in 1919 when reporters on the *Los Angeles Times* announced their astonishment at his sensational designs. More orders were brought in. For Fatty Arbuckle, Earl made what he later called 'the most streamlined vehicle anywhere', adding as an aside, '*and* it cost him $28,000!' For the early Western star Tom Mix, Earl made the sort of symbolic gesture that was to reoccur at different points in his career when he fastened a real leather saddle to the roof and painted the star's 'TM' logotype all over the unfortunate vehicle. In a monochrome industry colour was an

The original site of the Earl Automobile
Works on South Main Street, Los
Angeles.

important element in customizing and Earl's first experience in this field was a
comedian client who selected the colour of his car by pouring cream until the
coffee turned the particular tone of brown he had had in mind.

It was in these first 'streamlined' cars that certain elements of car styling which
were to dominate Earl's career began to emerge. Arbuckle's car was longer and
lower than those of his peers and the form was sensuously moulded, with junctions
of panels being made not by sharp abutments but by softly sculpted transitions.
There were expressive details too: motifs like landau irons recalled the days when
coachwork was for coaches, even if the irons were fixed and acted only as applied
decoration; and already some early designs were doing away with the primitive
running boards whose later obliteration from the face of the American motor
industry was to be declared the designer's greatest single formal innovation. The
three-piece windshield, even though the individual panels were all still flat,
already hinted at a mind which was questing to achieve wraparound glass. And in
a world where the mass market was getting black cars from Henry Ford, Harley
Earl was already supplying his cars for the stars in polychromed variety and in
very high degrees of finish.

One of the Earl company's most important customers was Don Lee, the Cadillac
distributor on the West Coast for whom the company did a lot of accident repairs
as well as some custom bodywork in the shop. In this primeval stage of the motor
industry distributors like Don Lee were more than just retail outlets, they were the
medium through which cars were translated to the customer, a fundamental part
of the industry's consolidated structure which Alfred P. Sloan was sketching on his
scratchpad in Detroit and deciding to call General Motors. These distributors were
as significant as the manufacturers, and many certainly outlived the evanescent

CELEBRITY CARS

The demand for cars with a special character for special clients allowed Earl, during his apprenticeship, to evolve a whole new vocabulary of form which he would later pass on to all of GM's manufacturing divisions. For each of the Hollywood stars who were his first clients—whether Jack Pickford or Roscoe 'Fatty' Arbuckle (LEFT)—Earl created an identifiable shape. It was the beginning of the perception that cars should be tailored for the individual consumer's needs—a principle which he later applied, with awesome success, to mass production.

producers who went bust when they found they had no way to distribute their goods. In 1919 Don Lee bought the Earl Automobile Works and in so doing acquired Harley Earl.

This acquisition gave to Don Lee America's first professional car stylist. It gave to Harley Earl direct access to top management in Detroit and, in particular, direct access to another extraordinary character, Lawrence P. Fisher, president of the Cadillac Division of Alfred Sloan's new conglomerate, General Motors. Fisher was to business administration what Harley Earl was to style: confident, imaginative and brash, a man whose taste for the pleasures of the flesh once led him to charter a couple of railway cars, fill them up with girls and champagne and go to Chicago to raise hell and lay cuties for an entire weekend. The great Cadillacs and their ritzy, lustrous, vulgar but impressive character go straight back to Fisher and to the day he said to Harley Earl, after a tour of the stars, starlets, fairways, pools, bars and bedrooms of Hollywood, 'Come with me, son, I've got a job for you.'

Fisher took Earl from Hollywood to Detroit and the move was like the trade of innocence for experience. Detroit was a very different place to Hollywood. An English traveller there noted, in distinction to the temporary nature of Los Angeles' most famous suburb, that Detroit's factories were awe-inspiring in their completeness and in the way intention was matched to form. He said the factories were in their own right 'works of art . . . stirring the imagination till it falls back exhausted'. It was a context of vigorous flux, ready for direction.

THE GENERAL

THE FORMATION OF GENERAL MOTORS

SINCLAIR LEWIS PUBLISHED HIS NOVEL *Arrowsmith* in 1925. It is a book concerned with transition and maturity, the adventures of the hero reflecting the changes which overtook America as it absorbed its industrial revolution and turned from being an Anglo-Saxon to an Italo-Slavic society. The car plays the role of significant motif throughout the novel and the primitive convertibles serve as symbols of careless youth: 'The thirty-eight miles an hour at which Cliff drove into Zenith was, in 1908, dismaying speed. . . . He stopped at the Fabulous Grand Hotel with a jar of brakes . . . his face had the pinkness of massage.' Towards the end of the book the car assumes the symbolic significance of being a trap laid by success for the innocent but aspiring hero who finds himself panicked in the 'soft and mothering prison . . . of a Buick sedan'. It was General Motors who made this change and Harley Earl who managed it for them.

To understand why Harley Earl was wanted by General Motors you have to understand why General Motors came into existence at all. In its early years the motor industry was an unsure investment: the E. I. Du Pont de Nemours Company of Wilmington, Delaware, did indeed become one of the biggest shareholders, but not with total conviction. The rules of growth and change which Alfred Sloan was to define had not yet come into play, and for a conservative American banking and investment world the automobile market did not seem an especially attractive investment. It was all flux, but that flux was tending towards consolidation.

Around the years of incorporation, when General Motors became an operating company with manufacturing divisions instead of a holding company for the car

LEFT America at leisure. *c.* 1924. By 1924. Henry Ford's philosophy
of supplying simple. generic products had made almost every
working citizen a real or potential consumer of the automobile.

LEFT ABOVE The 1923
Chevrolet was a second
generation automobile. The
first generation had been
motorized carriages, but now
the car had become a mature
consumer product. It was not
yet a vehicle of desire: the
car was still a simple tool
rather than an expression of
fantasy.

LEFT BELOW Louis Chevrolet
seen at the wheel of one of
his 1914 cars. The Chevrolet
car manufacturing concern
was bought up by Alfred P.
Sloan while he was
assembling the various
businesses that were to
become the General Motors
Corporation.

plants, a buying spree went on. General Motors bought the Guardian Frigerator Company (which later became Frigidaire), the Samson Sieve Grip Tractor Company, the Janesville Machine Company, the Doylestown Agricultural Company and, in 1918, Louis Chevrolet's car company. The acquisition of Chevrolet gave General Motors a car manufacturing division that in terms of volume and market appeal was to put it on a par with the mighty but simple Ford Motor Company, the market leader.

The twenties was a period of hectic and fundamental change in the automobile industry, when the business of making cars altered even more than it had after 1908 when Henry Ford introduced the low-dollar Model 'T' and defined the rules of the mass market game. Under Alfred Sloan, a dark-suited Michigan WASP who combined the organizational authority of the British Civil Service with the analytical powers of a Karl Marx, General Motors was martialled into becoming a challenger to Ford. In fact, under Sloan the General's policy was to wipe the Ford Motor Company off the face of the earth.

For a member of so conservative an organization, Sloan's views about change were remarkable: he relished it. He saw the General's position behind Ford, like everything else, as a business challenge. 'We had', he said, 'no stake in the old ways of the automobile business; change meant opportunity.'

On a larger scale, the advent of the 'talkies' and of broadcast radio in the United States was met by the same mixture of excitement and scepticism which the motor industry evinced before it entered its third and most dynamic phase. For his executives to understand where they stood in the park, Sloan analysed the three phases in the history of the automobile industry.

The first was the period up to 1908 when a rich privileged few had acquired

Before Harley Earl invented
the promotional Motorama,
America had no national
auto shows. In 1927, when
the Boston Auto Show (LEFT)
took place, the only
opportunity the consumer
had to review products of
rival manufacturers was at
privately organized
exhibitions, usually held in
hotels.

exclusive, hand-made horseless carriages. The second phase was the period during and after 1908 when Henry Ford realized the potential of the mass market, and his Model 'T' achieved hegemony. The third phase Alfred Sloan saw as belonging to General Motors: it was General Motors' mission to realize the mass *class* market. It would do this by offering not a generic garden variety car like the Ford, but a whole range of subtly graduated vehicles situated in the marketplace so that they could prise money off farmboys through to corporate executives.

During the twenties car ownership in America tripled to almost twenty million. With the basic transportation needs of the population virtually satisfied, the customer was expected to buy vehicles for reasons of status and symbolism as much as for getting to work. Painfully slowly, but always perceptively, General Motors management realized what was happening. It was a case study from an economics textbook which had not yet been written. They began to realize that something was happening to the private car, something which Henry Ford in his rush to satisfy universal demand had passed over – people were trading in their old cars and buying new ones. This was the first time in the history of the world that this had occurred: the first round of car buying was over. Although the evolution in the mechanical design of automobiles was slow, so that in all essentials the 1908 Ford was not hugely different from, say, the 1922 model, people were actually bringing in the old one and using it as a down payment on a new one. By about 1925 the majority of Americans were coming round to buying a new car for the second time.

Car production, like car ownership, almost tripled during the decade. It was good for business but the surge forward brought with it the danger of its own whiplash. Sensing the dangers of market saturation, General Motors' executives began inching their way towards a structural change in the nature of car design and manufacture which set the pattern for the entire industry until its collapse in the seventies. At a General Motors sales committee meeting during 1925 a paper titled 'Annual Models versus Constant Improvement' was tabled. They voted for the annual model. This meant that the world's biggest industrial organization in the world's richest country was voting for novelty instead of conservatism in its products. The unstated assumption was that each year's models should be superior to the last. Sometimes this had actually happened to be the case, but not always. In fact the engineering specification and the design had tended to get consolidated, and refined only piecemeal, but from now on each year's new cars would look different in pursuit of fresh dollars. It sounds familiar today, but it was a daringly novel conception in 1925. Without quite realizing it, without the necessary vocabulary, General Motors executives had summoned up the genie of *styling*.

The growth of the car industry and then the growth of car styling within the car industry were two phenomena inseparable from the history of the consumer society in America. In the United States the industrial revolution came later, and had more finite limits, than in Britain. If Britain's industrial revolution was all about heavy engineering, railways and cotton mills, America's was more concerned with mass production and with increased consumption. The end of mass immigration in 1921 meant that the pool of cheap, unskilled labour was limited, and this – together with the lessons of the First World War – was a hefty stimulus to the development of techniques of automated production. Although the economies brought about by standardized components made on a vast scale were a necessity for the war, they created the basis for huge economic growth in peacetime. The years of the birth of the private automobile as a democratic reality were the same years, 1919 to 1929, when industrial production in the United States increased by one hundred per cent. In 1929 there were three and a half million trucks registered in America; in 1903 there had been seven hundred.

Car bodies were amongst the last elements of the car to be standardized during the rush to create an efficient industry. Before Dodge's introduction of the all-steel enclosed body in 1923, most American cars had been convertibles and these convertibles all shared the same visual characteristics. Because they consisted of coachbuilt panels attached to a wooden frame on top of a separate and extremely rigid chassis, the finished bodies tended to be flat; if there was any curvature at all, it was not used for expressive ends, but rather as an expedient to make one flat plane in a certain direction meet another flat plane in an opposing one.

The impression that cars should be convertibles was very much enhanced by the success of Henry Ford's Model 'T', for whose construction the moving chassis assembly line was introduced at Dearborn in 1913. Henry Ford viewed the Model 'T' as an objectively desirable machine, entirely resistant to change and the whims of fashion, perfectible by virtue of enhanced efficiency in manufacturing. This was why they were any colour you wanted, as long as they were black. Model 'T's were meant to be generic products and they introduced a whole American generation to the democratic experience of independent motoring.

The contrast of Henry Ford to Harley Earl puts Earl's achievement into more startling silhouette. The one was a farmboy who knew at first hand the drudgery and loneliness of life in the rural states and produced his rugged and simple cars to make people free. Earl came from Hollywood, where he had been handcrafting custom-built cars for the stars. That Harley Earl was to supersede Henry Ford as

LEFT Model 'A' Fords on a transporter. Henry Ford's perfection of mass production forced his competitors to redefine the ground rules of the automobile industry. GM decided it needed style, so it acquired the services of Harley Earl.

an influence in Detroit was a metaphor of the change that overtook the whole American car industry in the twenties.

During the early years of trying to perfect the product, engineering had been an all-consuming concern of the manufacturers. The matter-of-fact advertising, mentioning features like the capacity of the generator and the degree of reliability which might be expected, all stressed this. A General Motors executive summarized the condition of the car before human factors of any sort (let alone visual and symbolic ones) were given attention: 'Engineering was the all-absorbing activity and the engineer was usually the dominant personality, often to the point of unreasonable insistence on having his ideas . . . followed to the letter regardless of manufacturing feasibility or ease of maintenance.'

Indeed, so obsessive had been the need to define and refine the basic product that customer appeal had been largely ignored. Alfred Sloan pointed out, 'For some reason, or other, it took us a long time to realize that the way to keep dry in a motorcar was to keep the weather out.' It was time to invent new bodies for the cars.

The mid-twenties Detroit manufacturers had all reached an acceptable level of refinement and reliability in their products, and functional characteristics ceased to be the chief selling point. There was now room for another element in the competition for sales: the Detroit car was about to fall out of the hands of the engineers and into the studios of the stylists. Ford acknowledged this when the timeless Model 'T' was replaced by the market-conscious Model 'A', and General Motors acknowledged it in a series of internal discussions which led to the appointment of Harley Earl as a full-time employee of the corporation.

At that time each of the five General Motors divisions was producing its own chassis, and these frames were then shipped to the Fisher body plant to have their coachwork added. This coachwork comprised running boards, fenders and mudguards, which are all separate components and which all sat, precariously upright, between the narrow tracks of the four wheels. In 1926 a typical General Motors car was 75 inches tall and 65 inches wide. Harley Earl's achievement was not only to change the shape of the car into a unified sculptural form but also to lengthen and lower it—always in appearance, often in fact. By 1963 the same typical General Motors product had shrunk to a mere 51 inches in height but had swelled to a massive 80 inches in width.

Harley Earl's first car for General Motors was produced at a time when the corporation was revising its model line so that it could offer a finely graduated spectrum of cars to meet every nuance of the mass class market. For the first time in the history of America's industrial revolution, products were going to be finely tuned for the consumer in a programme of activity which would later become known as a marketing strategy and which would be seen as the runes of Detroit. When he arrived in Detroit, Harley found the General's product line had crucial gaps, the most urgent one being between the $1295 Buick '6' and the $2985 Cadillac. The General abhorred a vacuum as much as nature, particularly a vacuum that sat there waiting to be filled by a competitor, and so, under the terms of the contract which Lawrence Fisher had offered Harley Earl to move east, the young man's assignment was to design a car that was to be a sort of people's Cadillac in order to fill that ugly $1700 gap between the most expensive Buick and the Olympian Caddy.

In fact this was to be the first car that the General caused to be *styled*. Sloan had mused once already about styling in 1921, and by 1926 the idea that appearance might actually affect sales was ripening colourfully in his meticulous mind. In a letter to his general manager at the Buick Division, Earl recalled that for the first Cadillac car he had ever had,

> . . . I purchased small wire wheels in order to get the car down nearer the ground and I never could see why, as motor car people, we have apparently been so loath to do a thing which contributes probably more to the appearance of the car from the attractive standpoint than any other single thing. . . . Slowly but surely we are . . . getting our cars down nearer the ground. . . . I am sure we all realize . . . how much appearance has to do with sales . . . and in a product such as ours where the individual appeal is so great, it means a tremendous influence on our future prosperity. . . . Are we as advanced from the standpoint of beauty of design, harmony of lines, attractiveness of color schemes and general contour of the whole piece of apparatus as we are in the soundness of workmanship and the other elements of a more mechanical nature?

It was just at the time of Sloan's musings about styling that Lawrence Fisher had discovered Harley Earl working at the Don Lee Corporation, busy blending all the running boards, fenders, trunks and headlights of the custom cars into coherent sculptural forms under their own power. What Fisher found Earl also doing was cutting the standard frames in half and adding sections in the middle to lengthen the cars, and therefore effectively lower them.

Sloan knew very clearly what he wanted and this was '. . . a production automobile that was as beautiful as the custom cars of the period'. This production automobile, aspiring to the condition of the exclusive cars of the stars, appeared in

March 1927 under the new brand name of La Salle and immediately it caused a sensation. Its appearance was entirely new: sharp corners had been excluded in favour of warmly curved junctions, disparate elements were harmonized into a unified whole and, as a hint of the chief concern in car structure that was to remain Earl's for the next thirty years, the silhouette had been lowered so that the car gave an impression of elegance and expressed a potential for speed. Later, in a telling piece of anthropomorphic analysis, Earl said he regarded the La Salle as 'slab-sided, top-heavy and stiff-shouldered', but this was just another way of saying how very far he had managed to take things in the interim.

Earl's designs for the new La Salle were state-of-the-art showmanship, employing a degree of theatre better known in Hollywood than in Detroit. He used all the custom car techniques, preparing full-sized models with nonpareil japan and then spraying them lightly with Duco so that they looked like glass. In making full-size presentation models Earl was already acknowledging the importance which scale was going to have for him in his career. He said later in a *Detroit Free Press* interview that 'the trouble with small models is that your eyes don't shrink with the model'. So he made them one-to-one and they sat there, glistening and novel, before Alfred Sloan's scrutiny.

The actual *design* of the La Salle was derived from the exclusive Hispano-Suiza, which Earl called the 'Hisso', even down to the badges. Sloan and his managers looked long and hard at the four different designs which Harley Earl presented. They were cool, these scrutineers, all trained in stock transfer, but they accepted the radical new designs, seeing in these Californian visions the very visual quality they had been seeking for the corporation ever since Sloan had first noticed back in 1921 that looks might help shift products. The acceptance of Harley Earl's designs for the new La Salle meant a number of things, but first of all it declared the creation of a native American school of car designers, while simultaneously wiping out the native American coachbuilding tradition.

Earl, who was not yet thirty-four, was exultant. He said, continuing the bar stool sports talk he had established for a medium of communication with Lawrence Fisher, that he felt like a quarter-back who had just thrown a pass for a touch-down; he had, and the simile needed extending. Harley Earl was so pleased that he returned to California. But Alfred Sloan was so pleased that he called him back.

With that pecksniff authority which characterized all of his pronouncements, Alfred Sloan declared on the strength of the La Salle that a decision had been made to 'obtain the advantages of [Earl's] talent for other General Motors Divisions'. What had been a one-off exercise in hiring a Californian body-customizer led to one of the major structural changes in the American manufacturing industry: General Motors Corporation decided to hire a stylist.

On 23 June 1927, Alfred Sloan announced to his sombre executive committee that he had the idea of establishing a special new department. Sloan lacked the vocabulary to say exactly what this department would do, so he said that it would supervise and coordinate the application of art and colour to the burgeoning product line of the General Motors Corporation. Alfred Sloan did not have an emotional approach to his business: he was not moved by cars. Indeed, the most excited he could get in describing them was to say that they were 'the dominant form of basic ground transportation in the United States'. When he created the Art and Colour Section and invited Harley Earl to head it, he was calm and sober, yet, as one employee suggested, the moment was rather similar in its cultural

————THE LA SALLE————

ABOVE Larry P. Fisher with Harley Earl, at the wheel of his 1927 La
Salle, outside the Copley-Plaza Hotel in Boston where the car was
launched. Fisher, who ran GM's Cadillac Division, met Earl during a
tour of California dealers. It was Fisher who invited Earl
to go to Detroit to work for the corporation.
OPPOSITE ABOVE 1927 Two-passenger Convertible Coupé.
OPPOSITE BELOW 1929 Five-passenger Sedan. The La Salle range,
conceived as a popularization of the premium Cadillac line, was
one of the US auto industry's first exercises in product planning.

implications, if on a much smaller scale, to that day in the fourth century when the Emperor Constantine decided as an act of expedience and on whim to turn the Roman Empire Christian. As one era ended, another began. The car was not going to be the same any more. To meet the demands of the first consumers of the automobile, Henry Ford produced fifteen million Model 'T's, cars with 'no more individuality than a carpet tack'. To meet the ever more sophisticated demands of the second generation of automobile consumers, the General hired Harley Earl. Just as the paint was drying on the Art and Colour signs, the Model 'T' Ford went out of production.

The new section began with fifty people – it was to grow to fourteen hundred people – and ten of the fifty were designers whom Earl was to train to interpret dreams of style for the public. His brief was a matter-of-fact one: he was to direct advanced production of bodies and to research ideas for new cars, the ones the public had not thought of yet. It was a general staff department but, as if to emphasize that it was inseparable from the actual business of manufacturing (rather as on a larger scale the American manufacturing industry has always had to be sustained by massive symbolic fantasies), the financing came from the General's metal-pressing and stamping Fisher body division.

Of art and colour, Henry Ford had had two things to say. As far as art was concerned, he said he did not care five cents for all the art the world had ever produced; as for colour, his customers' choice was restricted to black. Smart competition would force Ford to change his attitudes, but if his views at this time represented the Detroit consensus, it is not surprising that Harley Earl thought that his own new department had a 'sissy name'. Yet the title was important. The timing for it was right: it was six years since Alfred Sloan's internal memorandum had announced to his fellow executives that art and imagination had a part to play in the character and market position of cars, and now the stasis in the motor industry allowed the manufacturers to indulge in the luxury of choice the better to seduce the consumer. Ford found himself upstaged by the technology of the Du Pont chemical company, which offered its first choice of polychrome synthetic lacquer paints in 1924 and thus released the sombre Michigan WASPs from their chromatic inhibitions, introducing them to the promiscuity of colour and fashion and to a game which lasted forty years and for which they wrote all their own rules.

The creation of General Motors' Art and Colour Section, at exactly the same time as the first independent design studios were being established by advertising draftsmen, window dressers and set designers in New York City, was an important moment in the history of modern material culture. It was evidence of a widening appreciation that machines have life and that it is the designer's role to give form and expression to that life. This was exactly what Harley Earl had been doing on his own account in Hollywood when he was taking crude chassis, tarting them up and turning them into cars for the stars.

Settled in Detroit, Earl made one major innovation in design practice which changed the shape of cars forever. While before, coachwork had been 'sketched' in hammered metal, producing forms that were necessarily stiff and inorganic, Earl introduced the custom shop technique of using sculptors' modelling clay over wooden armatures. The use of this flexible material gave him the opportunity to create shapes which had a coherent, unified formal direction. To the horror of the accessory manufacturers, Earl was able to use clay and the new metal-pressing techniques to dispense with the trunk. This had been a strapped on afterthought to the coachwork and instead, Earl designed cars where the hood, cabin and trunk were all inseparable parts of an integrated form. The cars expressed for the first time an idea of style on behalf of the manufacturer, and for the first time gave to the customer not a contraption for travelling to and from the farm but a vehicle to symbolize his view of himself and the world.

The creation of a freebooting department whose brief was to fantasize was greeted with apprehension from the divisions in this heretofore conservative organization, dominated by development engineers and practical salesmen. One sales manager worried that if there was going to be a single Art and Colour Section under the direction of one man, then, surely, all the cars from all the divisions would end up looking the same. However, Earl would delegate: he had a team. He even went to Europe to search for talent, but came home and established what was to be the most influential school of American designers. Indeed, one of the draftsmen working on the La Salle was Gordon Buehrig, who later went his own way and designed the time-defying, although commercially unsuccessful, Cords. The department was a huge innovation and others' fears about it very soon seemed justified. Disaster struck: Art and Colour's first car was a lemon.

This was the Buick Silver Anniversary car, designed for introduction in 1929. It soon became known to the public as the pregnant Buick because of its awkward bulbous shape. Sloan dropped it from the marketplace just as soon as he could hustle a replacement, barely a year after its introduction. It taught Art and Colour and Harley Earl an unforgettable lesson. Sales of the Buick Division dropped by thirty-seven per cent, and Earl and his team learnt quickly to respect the public. Sloan interpreted the disaster in a way that made the episode seem like an efficient rehearsal for the introduction of planned obsolescence, and Harley Earl concurred. Sloan noted in a rueful tone that 'consumers could be prepared by measured steps for more radical changes in styling'. Too rapid a move clearly fooled and disorientated them, and from now on, once Earl had solved the problem of integrating Art and Colour into engineering, there would never be rapid moves in styling without preparing the public for change.

Earl rationalized the disaster as a lack of communication between his department and body engineering:

> I designed the 1929 Buick with a slight roundness both ways from the beltline highlight, and it went into production. Unfortunately . . . the factory pulled the side panels in at the bottom more than the design called for. In addition, five inches were added to the vertical height, with the result that the arc I had plotted was pulled out of shape in two directions, the highlight line was unpleasantly located, and the effect was bulgy. . . . I was unaware of what had happened until I later saw the completed cars. Of course, I roared like a Ventura sea lion but it was too late to keep car buyers from having a lot of fun naming the poor *enceinte* Buick . . .

It said something for the degree to which Art and Colour had been resisted by other divisions in the corporation that the car could go from concept to production without Earl being aware of the changes made to his design. But it was this car that taught Earl an ugly lesson which laid the basis for the total integration of Art and Colour into the General's hierarchy and which, eventually, gave Earl more influence in senior management than any mere engineer ever achieved.

THE IDEAS' RACE
THE INVENTION OF CAR STYLING

THE 1927 LA SALLE AND THE 1929 PREGNANT BUICK, the one a success, the other a failure, were the first expressions of the new mass class market in which the car was to be treated not as an outgrowth of the covered wagon but as a vehicle with its own character and purpose. The first mass market car to be styled was the 1933 Chevrolet with the new 'A' series body, a vehicle which can claim to be the first manufactured expression of Harley Earl's philosophy of automotive form. The exposed parts and projections were integrated into a sculptural whole, while the rear gas tank was incorporated with the trunk to make a 'tail'. For the first time, the radiator, a mechanical device intended to moderate the temperature of the engine coolant by exchanging heat, was not openly exposed to the airstream and dust and bugs—but was hidden behind a decorative grille. This single device was to be one of the chief ideas which Harley Earl gave to the generation of stylists who followed him.

The first steps were stumbling ones. The concept of styling, even where it was known, was not well understood, especially, in Harley Earl's interpretation, by the engineers. He had blamed them for the wrecking of the 1929 Buick. But despite his anger at the fiasco, the episode of the *enceinte* Buick taught Earl a salutary lesson: that you must not make sweeping, radical changes in production cars. Although he shrugged and asked acquittal for that car when questioned by the press, the Buick helped make the huge successes that followed possible. Teaching Earl to moderate the tempo of change in appearance so that he led the public, but only just, meant that the various technological changes which were occurring in the

LEFT 1935 Chevrolet at a Philadelphia gas station. By the mid-thirties, Sloan's General Motors had overtaken Ford as market leader and cars designed by Harley Earl dominated the streetscape in every American city.

KING EDWARD VIII's BUICK

Buick was always a speciality division, but with a custom-built car for Edward VIII in 1936 the Flint, Michigan, manufacturer achieved celebrity status. The commission came to Harley Earl through the King's contact with a Canadian dealer. The car was of great importance to Earl, and a monogrammed, bound album, with 'The King's Buick' tooled on the cover, left there when Earl retired in 1959, can still be seen at the Tech Center.

48

thirties could be fully understood before being translated into form, and the ill-considered or misconceived were avoided.

Chief amongst the technological innovations was the introduction by US Steel of the high-speed strip mill which by 1934 was providing sheet metal in 88-inch widths. This made the old half-steel half-fabric flat-top design immediately obsolete, and allowed Earl and his men to visualize a world of cars with sculpted 'turret tops'. It also meant that there was enough metal to play with when it came to fabricating wild new shapes for the dream cars which Earl invented to test the public's acceptance of new models before they were committed to production and, therefore, perhaps, committed to disaster like the poor Buick.

By 1937, Harley Earl had built up enough credentials within the corporation to have proved his point, and his Art and Colour Section became Styling. A new word thus entered the vocabulary of American car business. Styling's first job was to invent dream cars to act as vehicles for new ideas and tests for public taste. The dream car was the gilded token of what became known as planned obsolescence, although the people at General Motors never called it that. Since the sales committee paper of 1925 which inaugurated the concept of the annual model, the idea that regular change should be a part of production was built into the system and was not tested for forty years.

The first dream car was Harley Earl's 'Y' Job, although, like everything else he was responsible for, it was actually drawn by somebody else – in this case, one George Snyder. The 'Y' Job was a two-passenger sports convertible based on a standard Buick chassis and stretched to a little less than twenty feet in length. It was an experiment with visual ideas in automotive design that were deliberately in front of the *Zeitgeist*, or so Earl and his staff would have had you believe. It

ABOVE The 1934 La Salle Straight 8 was an early
expression of Earl's desire to make his designs
longer, lower and more sculpturally complex.
OPPOSITE ABOVE The 1938 Cadillac 60 Special was
the first car to show the razor-edged look
which Earl's assistant and successor as head of
Styling, William Mitchell, made his own.

sounded better than saying that this year's production was actually about four years out of date.

The 'Y' Job in fact incorporated some of the more successful styling idioms of the Chrysler Airflow, a car whose launch had been so unsuccessful that its manufacturer, in a surreal inversion of conventional industrial practice, was to make successive models progressively more conservative instead of progressively more radical. Going too far had frightened Chrysler into withdrawal; in Earl's case the same experience taught him to be cunning. But although the integrated forms and flush seams had been seen on the Airflow, the 'Y' Job was nonetheless a remarkable car, predicting by about twelve years some of the fads which were to dominate car styling during the fifties.

It was the first vehicle to emerge from General Motors' Styling which used Earl's visual imagination to the uninhibited full and in which the sculptural results of using the modelling clay were sensuous panels, bent in three planes. The car's features included electric windows, power-operated concealed headlights, a power-operated convertible roof, and an integral shape which, like the contemporary Citroën 12 of Flaminio Bertoni and the production Cadillac 60 Special of 1938, did away with running boards. It had wraparound bumpers, used to add semantic form as much as to provide considerable protection during bouts of acoustic parking; flush door handles, and the first horizontal grille for the radiator. This grille, along with the thirteen-inch wheels—small for the day—contributed heavily to achieving Earl's artistic end of making all his automobiles look longer and lower; if 1937 trends were extrapolated the 1965 Buick would be about the size and height of a tennis court.

When the 'Y' Job was introduced, there were no regular automobile shows on a

——— THE 'Y' JOB ———

The Buick-based 'Y' Job (OPPOSITE) of 1937 was the first dream car, a
type of vehicle which allowed the development of ideas and details
which were known to be too sophisticated (or too expensive) for mass
production. Recessed headlamps and a power hood became familiar
motifs and accessories during the fifties. With his dream cars, Earl
put ideas into three dimensions and built tomorrow today.
ABOVE Earl outside the San Francisco Civic Center with the 'Y' Job,
which he used as his personal transport.

G M COACH

37-PASS

Greyhound Lines

Scenicruiser

54

—— THE GREYHOUND BUS ——

The Greyhound Bus—a symbol of mobile,
democratic America, a generation after
Henry Ford's Model 'T'—was a product of
Earl's studios. Raymond Loewy was used
as consultant designer.

national scale in the United States so the public's reaction had to be pretested via public relations. A release declared that the 'Y' Job had 'made possible better looking, more advanced cars produced years ahead of the time they would appear in normal evolution'. The car was not frequently displayed. Instead, after the car was announced to the public in 1940, Harley Earl used it as his personal transport so that he could astonish members of the Question Club, the Recess Club, the Country Club of Detroit, the Grosse Pointe Club and the Yondatega Club with his mechanized panache.

The Second World War brought stagnation to car design. The 'Y' Job was next seen in 1947, when it was dusted off and reintroduced to give a direction to the cars of the fifties. But the war brought something else to Earl. That he had a vision which could direct the creation of cars with a coherent sculptural form and identity was already clear. Yet, although certain elements of his prewar cars included gestures and motifs derived from the sights at the Santa Monica race track, the 'Y' Job and the others, for all their presence and drama, lacked the element of detail and symbolism which made the cars of the fifties, America's Elizabethan age, so ruthlessly effective in extracting the last scintilla of cupidity and the last deferred-payment dollar out of the customer. The war gave Earl a source for the symbolic form, a taste for which had been modest before 1942 but under Earl's direction was to become a national craving in the fifties.

It was a war plane that did it, the Lockheed P38, known in Britain as the Lightning. This plane, sketched to a 1937 US Army Air Corps specification by Clarence (Kelly) Johnson of Lockheed – another visionary who climbed the corporate ladder to become a senior executive in a major US industry – was the object of a visit by Earl and his team to Selfridge Air Force Base, near Detroit.

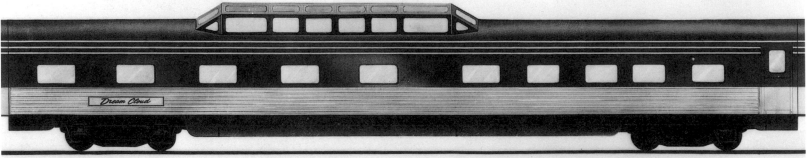

—— TRAIN OF TOMORROW ——

As vice president in charge of Styling, Harley Earl was responsible for the creative direction of every General Motors product, even the trains and the fridges. The 'Train of Tomorrow', of 1947, was to the railroad what the dream car was to the automobile: an exercise in material theatre to seduce the public.

After Cadillac, Buick was General Motors' most lustrous division and the one which received the second largest number of novel ideas. The 1947 Buick Roadmaster (LEFT) was one of the first of the division's cars to appear after the end of the war. As well as carrying over the essential form of the prewar 1942 model, it also employed some details from the experimental 'Y' Job. For 1957, Buick produced a longer, lower and neater Roadmaster (ABOVE) than the models of the late forties.

They got to see it because the General's Allison Division made the engines. It was under security when they saw it and no-one, not even Earl, was allowed to go nearer than thirty feet. This prevented them taking in all the radical details which the plane sported: its projectile-shaped nose, its cockpit greenhouse, its beautifully contoured streamlining and its twin tail booms. Not all of them, however. The admiring party led by Earl stood afar, and what they took in was the *twin tail booms*. At thirty feet, only the big details are noticeable and it was the tail booms that got through the broad gauze that was Earl's filter on the world of experience.

At the end of hostilities, just as the 'Y' Job was being dusted off for public showings, the first fresh design which Earl pulled out of the plan chest was as radical in its way as Kelly Johnson's pursuit plane. Earl even called it the 'Interceptor'. He was never one to deny the source of a good idea. From thirty feet he had soaked up the lines of the Lockheed plane and found the source of the style for the next decade. Those twin booms were to become the celebrated and then infamous fishtail fenders, or tail fins.

Yet at first Earl was not sure, not one hundred per cent positive. The 1948 Cadillacs were coming up for a new styling job. Immediate postwar cars had been carry-overs from the thirties, and the Cadillac, as the General's prestige division, was to get the benefits of new styling first. If a whole form or a certain detail proved successful on a Cadillac then, in conformity with the Darwinian principles respected and followed by the corporation, that same form or detail would be passed all the way down the product line. Although the idea of using the Lockheed tail fin on the first of the new style Cadillacs appears to have been Harley Earl's, when he presented Styling's work to other executives, it bombed. Earl was shaken and came back to his headquarters saying, 'Take that goddam fin off, nobody

wants it.' The designer on the drawing-board said no. Earl threatened to fire him. The designer on the drawing-board covered it up with a sheet of paper. Three days later Earl came back, said the idea was going over very well and added that next year they would make the fin bigger. It was a good idea. 1949 became Cadillac's best ever sales year.

Earl may not have realized what he was starting. What was little more than a raised rearlight on the 1948 Cadillac became more and more inflected and huge: Oldsmobile followed in 1949, Buick in 1952, Chrysler in 1955, Hudson, Studebaker and Nash in 1956, and Ford, perhaps in deference to the ideals and ideas of its founder who had wanted to achieve standardized products, held out until 1957. By 1959 the tail fin had become so grotesque a motif that the rear of the Chevrolet Impala looked like a fan dancer's tantrum and, in conformity with the Darwinian system, by the time the fin had spread from apex to base it was time to take it off the prestige Cadillacs, which appeared for 1960 as a model of poise and restraint.

The fin was one of the first elements in the ideas race of the fifties, the constant search for visual novelties to give the customers what Earl called a visible receipt for their dollars. He said that design was the entertainment business. To the marketing men the prestige which new motifs like the tail fin gave to a car was the crucial *non-price factor* which made that year's model a success. The concept of the non-price factor applied, of course, only to the customer. To Alfred Sloan all this art and colour was beginning to prove 'the dollars-and-cents value of styling'.

Earl's colleague and successor as vice president in charge of Styling, Bill Mitchell, saw the tail fin in the unembarrassed days of the fifties as an element in the mystic continuity of the Cadillac Styling department: 'The board is never

62

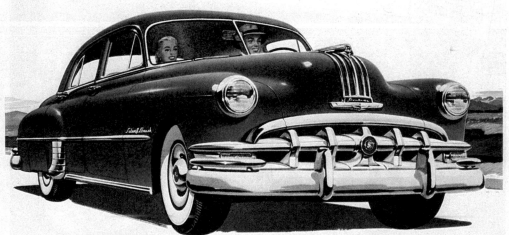

OPPOSITE GM advertising stressed the market segmentation of its divisions. The cars occupied what Tom Wolfe would later call 'statuspheres', but it could have been written 'status fears'. Pontiac, for instance, was more exclusive than Chevrolet, but was not supposed to compete with Cadillac. Copywriters chased very fine distinctions to find their Unique Selling Proposition. For Pontiac it was 'Silver Streak Styling'. The speed whiskers were the products of Virgil Exner's imagination, but the overall strategy was Harley Earl's. ABOVE 1947 Pontiac Torpedo.

LEFT The 1948 Proving
Ground Show displaying the
entire line of General Motors'
planned production for 1950.

65

erased in designing Cadillacs. If a fin is changed, the front end is not changed. If the front is changed, the fins are not touched. If the shape of the hood is changed, the grille is not monkeyed with.' In marketing terms, the invention of the tail fin for the first time brought real product identity to the back as well as to the front of the car. As Alfred Sloan remarked, 'Now you can have a Cadillac in the rear as well as in the front.'

Art had come to the aid of industry but at first the public did not buy the car and there was panic at General Motors. It looked like it was to be another pregnant Buick. Dealers declared that it was too radical. The first reported sales figures read LEMON, but almost overnight the mood changed. The 1948 Cadillac became a success with its public, 'either through their own discrimination or from advertising enticements', according to an editor of *Car Life* writing in 1954. The tail fin became identified with prestige and large amounts of disposable dollars. It acquired a reputation as the hallmark of a car that was 'well styled' and the car that it rode on defined General Motors' standards for at least ten years, providing a catalogue of motifs and inflections that could be used all the way along the General's huge product line so that the mass got class during the market boom of the fifties. The popular journals attributed Cadillac's success to styling and, therefore, to Harley Earl. It was the best of times.

The 1941 Buick Special Convertible Coupé (LEFT) was one of the division's last lines before the Second World War. The influence of Harley Earl's 'Y' Job was just coming through, but it was only with the first major postwar restyling of 1949 that the new forms of the future began to emerge. The Riviera Hardtop was introduced in that year, and in 1951 a four-door sedan (ABOVE) was added to the line.

THE GOLDEN AGE OF GORP

THE CARS OF THE FIFTIES

THE 1950S WERE AMERICA'S GOLDEN AGE, when it seemed that Alfred Sloan's prophecy of indefinitely increasing economic growth was going to be realized. In these Eisenhower years the coast-to-coast freeways were built, enabling the average family to exploit the potential of the automobile for the first time. In 1954, for instance, there were forty-seven million passenger cars registered in the United States, the highest concentration of them being in Wayne County, metropolitan Detroit. The motor city loved its darlings. US car production reached its highest ever point in 1955, the moment when Harley Earl's practice and philosophy of design reached its giddy peak.

Anatole Lapine, the present head of the Porsche Studio, worked at General Motors during the fifties. He recalled that:

> The assignment at General Motors for an executive in charge of the Styling Division consisted in being responsible for five million General Motors cars getting sold annually. The method that you elect . . . is yours! If you do not handle the job properly—if there are less than five million sold—your telephone will ring at midnight.

Harley Earl's sleep was never disturbed.

The basic technique of adapting production cars to American popular fantasies was for the corporation's Body Development Studio to develop the 'architecture' of a car, which would then be used across all five General Motors divisions. It was Harley Earl's job to differentiate between each product level, so that the fantasies

LEFT 1957 Cadillac Eldorado Brougham Coupé.
Derived from the Motorama cars of 1953–5, it was
the first American car to have quadruple headlights.

RIGHT The Cadillac Eldorado
of 1953 first appeared in the
Motorama for that year's
models. A reflection of the
$7750 sticker was that only
532 examples were sold.
Nevertheless. in its
exaggerated length and
lowness. as well as in details
such as the metal lid which
covered the lowered convertible
top. the 1953 car prefigured
many developments
of the rest of the decade.

this practical dreamer offered the Chevrolet customer were visibly and spiritually different from the highest dollar dreams offered to the more plutocratic owner of the Cadillac. This bizarre practice was realized by the Body Development Studio shipping its in-white structures of car architecture to the separate divisional design studios so that art and colour could be laid all over them and separate identities created for each of the General's divisions. Structural determinants of car architecture being what they are, the designer's freedom was restricted to the front and rear ends and the interior trim. Nevertheless, under the dinosaur gaze of Harley Earl, behind which lay a mind filled with the snazzy flotsam of a commercial culture, the General's designers achieved remarkable levels of differentiation which would have pleased the most pedantic medieval scholastic, let alone a shoe salesman from Des Moines.

Earl would wander around the studios making screwball suggestions or goofy wisecracks, or bawling someone out, before moving on. Later, the men at the boards were delighted when their boss commended them for solving the problem in exactly the way he had suggested. In fact, with Earl a suggestion amounted to a brief.

The creative procedures involved in designing new cars were theatrical and fantastic. To all new recruits to his staff, Earl, not a great reader, recommended Elbert Hubbard's *Message to Garcia*, a short text whose tone was somewhat like Baden-Powell's admonitions to British boy scouts in its moralizing fervour, but Earl would cheerily admit in successive and repetitive magazine articles that two of the chief influences on him had been Cecil B. DeMille, who taught him magisterial theatricality, and Al Jolson, who taught him how to judge the character of an audience. His office arrangements smacked of the theatre rather

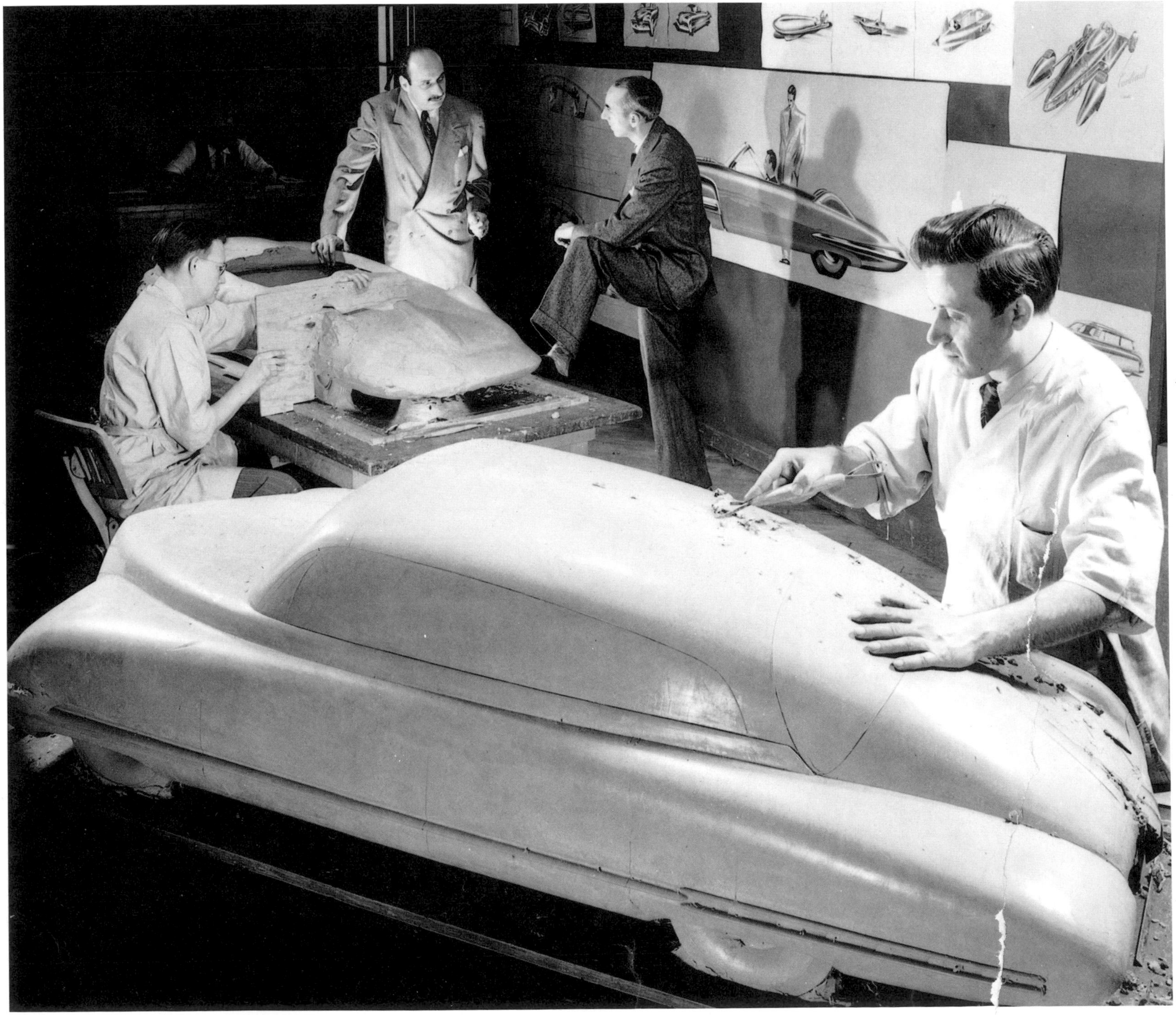

LEFT The chief innovation which Harley Earl brought from Hollywood to Detroit was the sculptor's technique of using clay to make models. This encouraged the creation of fluid, complex contours. Before Earl, models were made of wood; the use of clay gave rein to the designers' imaginations and the results were soon seen in metal.

than sound environmental design. He had a 'hatchery' where his bizarre ideas came to him, and in his hatchery he saw to it that the windows were blacked out — in case anybody could read his mind — that no telephone was connected and that there was a misleading name on the door so that his concentration might not be interrupted by a trivial intrusion into the turbulent id of a General Motors vice president.

In practical terms Harley Earl supervised five car design studios, one for each General Motors division, as well as twelve special studios. Each studio manager reported to a director of Styling who in turn reported to Harley Earl. He, with a degree of responsibility for design unique in American industry then and now, reported only to the corporation's president.

The way Earl managed his team went right back to the days when he was manager of the Californian custom body shop. In the shop he had been a coordinator and a kibitzer, and in his first consultant job for Cadillac he had acted in these roles, to which he also added the new role of free-ranging talent scout. He was not a draftsman or a visualizer, but he got his job done by a continual process of critique and commendation. He kept a competitive creativity going among his staff by having a locked door policy for each of the five divisional studios so that none knew what the othes were doing. Only Earl had the key.

The process which Earl established for getting a concept through to production has not changed to this day. At a policy meeting the corporation's president and his top management would decide to introduce a new body line on a particular year's Chevrolet, Pontiac, Buick, Oldsmobile or Cadillac. Earl and the other vice presidents, with responsibilities for Engineering, Research, Manufacturing and Finance, would all be present and so would the general manager of the particular manufacturing division involved. After the meeting Harley Earl would go away and brief his number two, the director of Styling, with the head of the divisional studio and the Advanced Body Studio both being present.

The studio heads would then meet with the body engineers to discuss the question of how any new development in the body engineering would either enhance or restrict their freedom of direction. The 'hardpoints' would be established – the unchangeable coordinates of passenger cell volume, ground clearance and overall length – from which a seating buck (a type of wooden jig) can be assembled to assess the ergonomics.

At this stage, the search for design enters the 'broad brush' phase. Harley Earl would review all the sketches from the drafting boards and select certain ones for further development; others would be consigned to the file marked 'bin'. Now full-scale concept sketches would be generated, the Advanced Body Studio concentrating on the general theme suggested by Earl's selection of sketches from the board, and the divisional manufacturing studio working up the expressive details of the front and rear ends, lights and roofline. If all went well, the design committee would oĸ the basic concept, and the divisional studio would finalize the telling details which give market differential to the finished car, so a Chevrolet looks different to a Cadillac even though it might share pressings and components.

The next step would be to translate the approved concept sketches into three-dimensional clay models. While the models were being fabricated, the clays would be continuously modified as visual and sculptural problems which could not be anticipated even on large drawings became apparent in three dimensions. To record how work was progressing, a full-scale linesdraft drawing would be made and updated as the clay was modified.

The resulting full-size clay model would be reviewed by top management and, if approved, a full-scale fibreglass model would be made, using the clay as a male mould. The fibreglass model would be given a realistically high finish, so that when it was wheeled around in natural light, management could assess the way highlights occur on the panels and how light and dark interact.

If the car was approved at this stage, then the decision would be made to go with it . . . and some unformed concept brewed up in the hatchery by Earl from something he saw on a street in Italy, read in an in-flight magazine, heard a colleague say his wife had remarked, or saw on television, was on the way to becoming one of America's master products in pressed metal.

Earl conducted the design process with a mixture of discretion, emotional violence and bizarrerie. He is said to have been a diffident speaker in public but to have known no equals in an internal meeting, where, in a perfectly judged theatrical performance, he would discomfort opponents with outlandish suggestions made with nary a quiver of self-doubt. Once he suggested to executives of US Steel that they should think about getting round to making transparent metal, and he would make the case for this, or any other stupid programme, without equivocation. There would be a hush, perhaps of embarrassment, often of awe; he would look slowly round the studio and, with a display of perfect reasonableness, would gently solicit an opinion about what he had just declaimed. Then he would say with a significant and terrifying pause after the fifth word, 'If any of you disagree . . . stand up so we can all get a look at the sonofabitch.'

The source of Earl's ideas about what to apply to the front and rear ends of the architecture which the Body Development Studio wheeled over to him was in his

——THE LE SABRE——

The Le Sabre show car derived its name from the
F86 Le Sabre jet. Modelled in clay during 1949, the Le
Sabre was built as a running car in 1951. It was the use
of the clay modelling technique which helped to give
the car its exceptional phallic jelly-mould appearance.
Le Sabre was the first car to feature the panoramic
wraparound windshield. A particular favourite of
Earl, he used it as personal transport (LEFT) around
the Grosse Pointe country clubs which he frequented.
The car never went into production, but it donated
many of its details—as well as its name—to GM lines
throughout the fifties. Eisenhower travelled in a Le
Sabre while NATO commander in Paris.

early dream cars. As soon as the war was over he began thinking about how to continue the tradition which he had begun with the 'Y' Job; economic circumstances having improved and general conditions being more propitious he knew he could now go further. The first significant dream car of the postwar years was the astonishing Le Sabre xp–8, a phallic jelly-mould of a car with aeroplane nozzles and details, which Earl named after the f86 Sabre jet serving the US forces. Earl, regardless of what the sociologists said about cars displaying your sexual fears, steered this awful tool around Grosse Pointe as his personal transport, leaving friends and colleagues at country clubs throughout Michigan astonished at his style.

Unlike the 'Y' Job, Le Sabre had no standard parts, but like the 'Y' Job it was a further step in Earl's lengthening and lowering philosophy and, again like the 'Y' Job, it incorporated features, most notably the image of the aeroplane and the wraparound windshield, which were to spread themselves all over the General's product line during the next decade.

The wraparound windshield in particular became a significant motif in car styling, changing the appearance of the car's whole upper structure. The hold this visual device had over an entire American generation illustrated the extent to which a public experienced in the business of consumption could apply subtle degrees of social evaluation to degrees of curvature in glass. With the panoramic windshield you were fashionable, without it you were *démodé*.

Fashionable or not, the wraparound windshield, like many of Earl's innovations, eluded the comprehension of the General's engineers, whom Earl had now subdued as effective rivals in the ideas race for the public's soul and its dollars. The engineers at the Libbey-Owens-Ford glass company were so confounded by the precise shape of the curved windshield Earl had instructed them to fabricate that they failed to find a mathematical formula to define the actual path the Veep wanted the glass to follow. The numbers to which Earl paid homage were not those known to Pascal, but rather those tested by Gallup. The poor engineers found that they could not make a curved windshield which did not offer the consumer deformation of the image ahead. Earl did not flinch and they had to sashay between his inflexible demands and the ASA code requirements. They were reduced to making the first batch by hand, but this did not bother Earl and when he was actually able to *prove* the demand, the benighted technicians at Libbey-Owens-Ford in fact managed to arrange to make them in series. They did not manage to improve the vision but they did get the windshields made in large numbers and, like a metaphor of the whole of the 'golden age of Gorp', the demands of the market which Earl created overrode the simpler laws of science.

Earl liked to take science at a superficial level. It is likely that the very idea of the wraparound panoramic windshield was derived from the bubble canopy of the Lockheed P38 which he so deeply admired from a distance. He loved planes in general and he tried to work into Le Sabre, and the production cars that followed, an impression of speed derived from the planes he had seen poised for flight on airfields across the States. He liked planes because they conformed to his ideas about cars looking longer and lower. He liked the impression of alertness and speed which the new tricycle undercarriages gave to planes at take-off. He did not want his cars to look as though they were sitting up and begging, nor as if they were hunkering down digging for woodchucks, and for this the craft of the air were his inspiration.

Once, travelling across the country, he found a picture of a Douglas Skyray in an

—— 1953 AND 1954 SERIES 62 CADILLACS ——

American usage allowed that the Cadillac had 'the best styling in the industry'. As the General's premium product, margins were such that plenty of designers' time was available to dream up the styling features which became the customer's visual receipt for the price he paid. Certainly Cadillac design details slid down the sides of the pyramid of the American auto industry. The tail fin, which was first seen on the 1948 Sedanet (a divisional coinage for coupé), became progressively exaggerated as the designers under Harley Earl worked their way higher and higher up the tightening helix of visual invention which the pursuit of novelty demanded.

OPPOSITE 1953 Cadillac Series 62 Hardtop. ABOVE Harley Earl posing with the successive 1954 models. When introduced, the 1954 Series 62 retailed at $3933.

LEFT The interior of the
1954 Cadillac brought the
application of aircraft
imagery in car design to a
new high level.

in-flight magazine and he stared at it for maybe an hour. He liked it. 'It was a
striking ship,' he said, so striking indeed that he tore the page out of the magazine
and put it in his inside pocket. When his travelling companion asked what he was
going to do next year, Earl was only momentarily quietened. Then he slapped his
breast pocket and said, 'I have it right here.' Later he added, 'I was only answering
the banter in kind. Then bingo, I decided I had kidded myself into something.'

Earl's unfortunate experiences with the 1929 Buick had taught him a colourful
form of caution, but new experiences were confirming that visual novelty was an
important inducement to sales. The formula was a nicely balanced one and it
resulted in what was later called planned obsolescence. It was fundamental to the
American economic system and even reluctantly acknowledged by Henry
Dreyfuss, the most conservative of American industrial designers, who was
responsible for the timeless 1933 Bell telephone. Dreyfuss remarked that the
designer 'must be able to anticipate the public's desires, yet guard against being
too far ahead. . . . Thus far he has kept his creations paced in a way that always
gives the public something just a little ahead that it can continuously reach for.'

This was Harley Earl's job, to offer the customers visual receipts for which they
could constantly strive, a concept which had been implicit ever since Alfred Sloan
had persuaded his executive committee to vote for annual model changes instead
of slow and steady improvement of a substantial design. Sloan explained: 'The
changes in the new models should be so novel and attractive as to create demand
for the new value and, so to speak, create a certain amount of dissatisfaction with
past models as compared with new ones.'

This meant that in 1951 Harley Earl was already driving around in what would
be the production car of 1954. His job was to create that dissatisfaction which,

—— 1954 NOMAD ——

ABOVE The production Chevrolet Nomad station wagon alongside a Nomad dream car (foreground) of 1954. This GM factory photo is a clear demonstration of the development principles which ruled Earl's views: he thought it was inevitable that, year by year, cars must become lower and longer in order to meet the public's increasing appetite for novelty and speed. Eventually the production Nomad became so low that, for the first time, even a man of average height could see the roof. Earl abhorred the wasted opportunity of undecorated metal, and so he grooved it. RIGHT 1954 Nomad dream car.

OPPOSITE The Nomad dream car was displayed at the 1954 Motorama, Earl's masterpiece of revelation in his role as industrial impresario; he mixed dream cars with production lines in a miasma of glittering form. As one Earl apprentice remarked, this was the age when 'we laid on chrome with a trowel'. The Motorama was like a vision of planned obsolescence telescoped, though Earl preferred to call it the dynamic economy which 'carried the standard of living of the people of America to the highest level ever enjoyed by human beings. . . . You will never know what the industrial products of the future are going to be like, but the secret is to keep trying to find out. . . .'

LEFT 1954 Chevrolet Corvette. The glass fibre Chevrolet Corvette was America's first modern sports car and the most powerful expression of Harley Earl's ideas about car syling. Conceived as a response to the imported MGS and Jaguars, the Corvette reached the market in 1953, less than two years after Earl and chief engineer Ed Cole had begun the design process. Earl told his design team to 'go all the way and then back off': they did not back off much. The irresistibly sensuous and dramatic Corvette derived some details from its aunt – the Cadillac – and others from imported Ferraris, but it achieved an identity all of its own.

uncharitably interpreted as waste through over-consumption, became an essential mechanism of the American economy and would lead the public into an ever-tightening helix of invention, seducing it year by year.

As far as Harley Earl was concerned, the best designs got responses in the form of cheques. He wrote in 1954:

> Most Americans are at least a little excited over the appearance of new-model automobiles every year. This is where I must leave you. I cannot get aboard because, considering the share of all the cars my company produces, the odds are almost even that your new car is one I designed myself and put out of my life at least twenty-seven months ago. Because of my job I have to live two or three years apart from a great American interest. I can't talk to the neighbors about their cars with anything like fresh enthusiasm. . . . Consequently I have to know more about you than you do about me. I do. For one thing, I know that car buyers today are willing to accept more rapid jumps in style than you were twenty years ago. This suits me because I believe we are entering an era of major design improvements. The further we move away from the old concept of the automobile as a motorized buggy the greater the emancipation of design.

Earl's dream cars had had the effect of bringing forward the public's taste for change so that they wanted today styling features which the General's consumer research had earlier showed they would only accept tomorrow. In an official speech called 'Remarks on Industrial Design', Harley Earl offered his own socio-historical interpretation:

> Markets become highly competitive and to compete successfully for buyers'

LEFT Harley Earl commissioned General Motors' incredible Tech Center from the Michigan-resident, father-and-son team of Finnish architects, Eliel and Eero Saarinen. Built on a 900-acre site for $125,000,000 at Warren, twelve miles northeast of downtown Detroit, the Tech Center was the architectural expression of Alfred P. Sloan's ambition and optimism. As much as the cars, it was a symbol of America's confidence during the Eisenhower years. In a photograph to mark the opening ceremony in 1956, dream cars are lined up in front of the Styling Auditorium, together with regular products from each of the General's five divisions.

dollars, manufacturers had to make more than a good product . . . they had to make them *look* attractive to the shopper. The answer was good design . . . not just design, but *good* design.

This American concept of 'good design' was absolutely different to the austere, moral, European commodity which went by the same name. In Europe, 'good design' was fundamental to a healthy social system; in Harley Earl's America it was fundamental to a healthy economy. Earl liked to think of it as *dynamic obsolescence* and he also thought it had a remote social purpose in making near-new cars available to the less well-off at used car prices, so that people further down the economic structure could buy cars they could not otherwise afford as a mass of new car buyers indulged in the annual model change.

To Earl, the successful creation of ever more dynamic obsolescence was the greatest challenge to the practising designer. The advice he offered to the prospective industrial designer was: 'You will never know what the industrial products of the future are going to be like, but the secret is to keep trying to find out.' A fellow General Motors executive described the process smartly when he said of the rapid succession of models, 'We have not depreciated these old cars, we have appreciated your mind.'

It was inevitable that this increasing sophistication in marketing policy would lead to an increase in consumer choice. Indeed, so varied and subtle did the process of tailoring cars to the individual consumer become that at one time in the fifties the Ford Motor Company, always a little way behind the General, was offering no fewer than four completely separate models of full-sized cars. This whole policy was so distant from the European ideal of objectively quantifiable

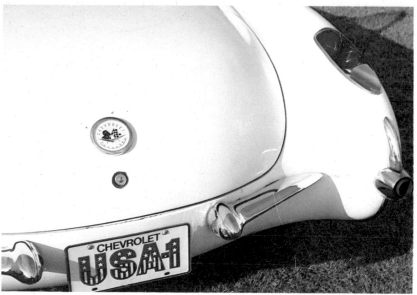

ABOVE AND LEFT 1956 Chevrolet Corvette. Earl's sports car was based on rocket ships and on distant memories of the Italian coachbuilding he had seen at the Paris Auto Show. Immediately the car dug a trough in the American imagination because its shape seemed to scream speed, sex and sunshine. But the engineers did not do Earl's dramatic designs justice: the sluggish Corvette almost died a year after its birth because it was neither luxurious enough for the *boulevardier* nor fast enough for someone who had owned an MG. Earl's team did, however, create a body style strong enough to resist major changes in mechanical specification.

OPPOSITE The 1953 Buick Skylark was produced for the division's golden anniversary. It was an entirely characteristic Harley Earl styling exercise. Created by cutting, chopping and lowering another car, the Skylark achieved exclusive looks. Although it sold less than 2000 examples, it was an innovation in the industry: Harley Earl had created the first 'personal' sporty car—later to become, with the Ford Mustang, an industry norm.

LEFT 1956 Cadillac Sedan
de Ville. Although most
American customers must
have been unaware that a
'sedan de ville' was a
designation derived from
traditional coachwork
practices, the name became
etched in the popular
imagination as a type of
luxury car.

'good' design that the marketing policy which Earl had established through his dream cars became known in Germany as 'Detroit Machiavellismus'.

Through the use of colour and materials, increasing choice in specifications and flexible assembly line techniques, by about 1957 the American consumer could order a car straight from the factory gates that was virtually custom-built. As one Yale physicist pointed out, the Chevrolet Division of General Motors alone was offering so many different body styles, engine options, transmission variants, trim colours and accessories that the number of variants available seemed likely to exceed the number of atoms in the universe, thereby putting Harley Earl one step in front of God in the chain of command.

The manufacturers laid on chrome with trowels during this period. The two most characteristic cars of the era were both Chevrolets, and each began as a dream car at one of Earl's Motoramas, the car festivals he invented in 1952. Inspired by his early acquaintanceship with Cecil B. DeMille, Earl used the Motorama to bring the car into the theatre of life. Regularly he attracted half a million innocent punters to gawp at his creations there and, being careful to notice their responses to his whims of steel, he used the shows as free opinion polls. Both the Chevrolet Corvette, America's first sports car, and the Chevrolet Nomad, America's first modern station wagon, emerged from speculations which Earl had caused to be designed and put on pedestals at a Motorama.

His general advice to stylists on the board was to 'go all the way and then back off', although with the Corvette it is hard to reconcile the results with this cautionary maxim. Promiscuous use had been made of symbolism, derived from Earl's usual sources as well as from exotic stock such as the Ferrari, which donated via Earl's licence its radiator grille to the Corvette's egg-crate harmonica intake.

ABOVE 1958, a year of recession in the automobile industry, was
the year when Chevrolet introduced a new model, the Impala.
The car began as a sub-series of the famous Bel Air, but soon
emerged to become Chevrolet's chief product line. Visually it
featured motifs first seen on Cadillacs, but adapted for the
coarser and simpler tastes of the mass market.
LEFT The 1957 Chevrolet Bel Air, named after a suburb of Earl's
native Los Angeles, became an object of veneration for
American youth. It was this car, powered by a 270 hp
fuel-injected lightweight v-8, that made Chevrolet's reputation
with the street racers.

LEFT The Pontiac Club de
Mer dream car of 1956 was
like a figurative metaphor of
America in the fifties: the
associations of the name and
the details evoked a
cosmopolitanism that was
superficially attractive but
ultimately colourless. As a
Californian, Harley Earl had
to produce a vision of the
future to replace a missing
sense of the past.

Immediately it appeared it defined the real purpose of the sports car. As a vehicle
for going round bends very fast under feline nervous control it was a non-starter:
its bus tyres lacked adhesion, its barge suspension made it feel like a raft in a swell,
and its two-speed automatic transmission responded to the driver's commands
with the sensitivity of Hoover Dam sluices. But as a boulevard cruiser, a car which
wore its pretensions on the outside instead of in the crankcase, like prissy
European designs, the Corvette was to the car what *Gone With the Wind* was to
weepy movies.

There were, of course, consequences to Earl's restless search for imagery to add
to form, for instance the lengthening and lowering policy. Earl was keen on
lengthening and lowering because 'my sense of proportion tells me that oblongs
are more attractive than squares, just as a ranch house is more attractive than a
square, three-story flat roof house or a greyhound is more graceful than an English
bulldog'. This policy of formal attenuation was so effective that by 1954 even so-
called utility vehicles like the Nomad station wagon had become so low that an
average-sized man could actually *see* the roof, although at six foot four inches Earl
himself had been able to see it quite a few new models back. Earl found that he
could not tolerate this untreated sheet of pressed steel which was now visible for
the first time. He probably feared that competitors would catch up and do
something with theirs first. He was not gaining the absolute maximum of effect
from his medium, the first time this challenge had ever been levelled at him. His
policy of lengthening and lowering had exposed a weakness in his conceptions: the
car had a dull roof, a mere bit of flat metal to keep the weather out and the sides
together. So what was his answer to the problem? 'We grooved it.' In the 1954
Motorama the Chevrolet Nomad station wagon got fluted pressings on its roof, and

LEFT 1958 was the last year
when GM produced distinct
body shells for its separate
divisions and immediately
Oldsmobile became a brand
in search of a character. The
1958 Super 88 had many
details from earlier

Motorama specials, but it
failed to win the admiration
of native critics of styling:
the correspondent for *The
Consumer's Guide* said that
the four chrome strips on the
rear fender looked like a
caricature of musical notation.

99

ever since non-structural corrugations have been an established part of the car designer's repertoire.

The Motorama itself had results. It was obvious that with his dream cars Earl was achieving huge successes in public relations and he was not at all reluctant to capitalize on them. His next step was to domesticate the Motorama and remove the business of designing cars from the Parnassus where he and his colleagues dwelled and pass it over to the folk living below.

Some time earlier, Harley Earl had noticed women. In fact, in 1917 he had married one of them, a girl called Sue Carpenter. It took him thirty-nine years, but by 1958 he was beginning to think that women might, alongside airplanes, have a role to play in car design. He would not adapt them *en bloc* to his designs, although any amateur Freudian was able to notice that the more evocative curves, folds, tucks and orifices of Earl's cars bore curious resemblances to the secret parts of women's bodies. Earl would have none of that. He decided to give women jobs instead. 'They don't realize', he declared, 'how many of our ideas come from the public and the aviation industry. And make no mistake about it, America's women have a lot to say about what they want in the new family car.'

This was the time before it was actionable for the vice president of a major manufacturer to remark that he was replacing cord with nylon for car seats so that his women customers would not wrinkle their skirts or get static on their stockings so that their loins ached.

Earl had always been keen on youth. In the late 1950s the average age of his stylists was under thirty and while it was nobody's secret that the men he looked for had 'gasoline in their blood' and that he found them lurking at drag strips, the damsels of design he went out and employed seemed to have something else,

THE FIREBIRD MODELS

Harley Earl's first cars in the Firebird experimental range appeared in the Motorama of 1954. They exceeded in every degree of imaginativeness and impracticality the regular Motorama show cars, and were touching evidence of the conviction and naiveté which were the two main forces of Styling at GM under Harley Earl. At one level, the use of the gas turbine appears to suggest an interest in the use of advanced technology, but the cars were loaded with redundant imagery and details. Now it takes an effort of imagination to see the cars as vehicles carrying prospective ideas for production; they were designed at a late stage in the history of American car styling.

OPPOSITE ABOVE Harley Earl with Firebird I in the Arizona desert, 1954. OPPOSITE BELOW Firebird II, 1956. ABOVE Firebird II. LEFT Firebird III, 1958.

LEFT The 1959 Cadillac
Fleetwood brought the tail
fin to its most extreme form
of development.

possibly Chanel, in their blood and he found most of them at Brooklyn's famous
Pratt Institute.

They were to provide a fashion show for Mr Earl, a show whose taproots went so
deep into the temporary obsessions of American fashion that they made Earl's
own Motorama entries look like disinterested scientific research. Earl brought
these smart and extremely WASP young ladies, with names like Vanderbilt and
Ford, away from their bridge tables, where, it was said, at least in the *Detroit
Sunday Times*, that all they discussed were frocks, recipes and children, into his
Tech Center so that they could let their psyches do the talking.

It seemed that although car talk was a late starter in comparison to bridge,
recipes, frocks and children, it was becoming more significant among the bobbed
and frocked alumni of Harley Earl's distaff staff. He decided to let them have a
fashion show of feminized cars at the Motorama for the 1959 model year.

The male designers with gasoline in their blood were apprehensive that these
twittering females would trivialize with chintz their hunky aeromorphic
barouches and add doodads rather than false vents, chrome whiskers, tail fins,
pseudo-heraldic badges or false gun ports. Earl, knowing a good thing and
backing a Neanderthal hunch, was with the women all the way. He rebuked his
restive male staff when he declared, with submerged Hollywood imagery, that 'the
damsels of design have won their spurs with this 1959 collection'.

The women actually got to feminize not only the cars and their accessories, but
also the names, romping like coursers through the level just below the surface
swamp of American aspiration, cupidity and psychic fear. Ruth Glennie did a
Corvette called Fancy Free in which unfortunate car, to complement the silver,
olive and white leather trim, she provided four sets of slip covers to change with

RIGHT Motifs which first appeared on Motorama show cars then appeared on GM cars for the American market and were finally passed on to the poor relations abroad. Vauxhall Motors of Luton was an English car firm which had belonged to GM since 1925. The 1959 Cresta and Victor show how Earl's ideas – somewhat diluted for English taste – became a familiar part of British life. The Cresta (left) was derived from the 1954 Pontiac Strato Streak dream car. Maurice Platt, Vauxhall's chief engineer at the time, said that the engineers 'hated Earl's guts because he added weight'. He added many other things besides.

104

the seasons and, in an unguarded although prophetic moment of generalized social concern, incorporated retracting seat belts to restrain the freed fancy. Ruth Glennie's colleague Jeanette Linder called her version of the Chevrolet Impala the Martinique and in it she put three-piece fibreglass luggage, designed to match the pastel-striped upholstery.

All these cars were intended to meet the needs of the newly emergent and short-lived 'fashionable career woman'. For instance, Marjorie Ford did a Buick called Shalimar, painted in royal purple and kitted out with a removable cosmetic case built into the armrest and a dictating machine on a swinging arm, fixed into the ample glove compartment. Sue Vanderbilt, a pretty twenty-four-year-old brunette from Larchmont, New York, did two cars. The first was a Cadillac. Not satisfied with the manufacturer's ample provision of names for the Cadillac Eldorado Seville, she wanted to add Baroness as well. According to the *Chicago American* Miss Vanderbilt preferred subdued colours which 'permit the occupant to shine', but she was licentious with accessories, which included a black mouton carpet, a phone, and a pillow and lap robe in black seal fur for the rear passengers. With her second car she betrayed a taste for the Teutonic and named it Saxony. Her Saxony had a dictaphone in the central armrest and partitions were thoughtfully provided in the glove compartment so that when the fashionable career woman lurched into a corner, the doodads, chintz and other contents would not surge.

Marjorie Ford followed the predilections of her sorority damsels of design, making her Buick a custom colour, in her case flaming orange. Expressing heaven knows what psychic urge, she had binoculars and a camera locked away in a padded compartment. In the flaming orange Buick you would also find, to use the

—— 1957 AND 1959 CADILLACS ——

ABOVE 1957 Cadillac Eldorado Biarritz.
OPPOSITE ABOVE 1957 Cadillac Park Avenue Sedan.
OPPOSITE BELOW 1959 Cadillac Eldorado Biarritz Convertible.
To the prosperous GM customer these Cadillacs offered not just
a means of transport, but the suggestion of an entire way of
life and system of values. Earl once said: 'You can design a
car so that every time you get in it, it's a relief – you have a
little vacation for a while.'

melodramatic imagery of the time, a transistor tube radio in a carry-out console. Apparently cubby holes were going like gang-busters with the damsels, and the last sister to produce, Peggy Sauer, also had a little shrine of concealment in her Oldsmobile, perhaps to counteract the all too noticeable effect of the car's exterior paint and trim, which Miss Sauer had caused to be metallic rose on the metal, with red and black interior leather relieved by tasteful plaid inserts.

This fashion show, which was widely reported in the American press, was a summary and conclusion to Earl's career as a designer. In his instruction to 'go all the way and then back off' it is interesting to consider what might have been left behind. Indeed, although the doodads and chintz and matching umbrellas were all amusing trivia, the damsels also introduced retractable self-adjusting seat-belts, door warnings and luggage straps. Earl was impressed that their human factors research not only went beyond the potential of stocking snag hazards on gear shifts, but into areas of ergonomic concern he had never anticipated. It was, after all, less than four years before the Chevrolet Corvair, designed by Earl's successor William Mitchell as a responsible, sophisticated car, had the accident which unleashed the Krakatoa of environmental protection and car safety legislation which killed the open car and ended the great liberal phase of American design.

Earl was at the end of his career and perhaps he sensed it. Apocalyptically he gasped, after a view of the breathtaking achievements of the damsels who had added ergonomics to the doodads, 'I believe the future for qualified women in automotive design is virtually unlimited. . . . I think in three or four years women will be designing' (pause) 'entire automobiles.' And the gasoline in the blood would turn to scent.

——1959 IMPALA——

The structure of General Motors
followed Darwinian principles.
The tail fin. which began as a
Cadillac detail in 1948. had by
1959 spread to the lower orders of
the species. When it hit the
proletarian but aspiring
Chevrolet Impala it had reached
ridiculous proportions: the rear
deck was big enough to take a
small plane. while the fins
themselves looked like a fan
dancer's tantrum. The Darwinian
metaphor holds good. since the
public found the '59 Impala
excessive: in later years the
tail fin became more and more
restrained until eventually it
became extinct.

GARDEN VARIETY AMERICA

HARLEY EARL'S LAST YEARS

IN 1958, THE YEAR OF THE FEMINIZED MOTORAMA, Harley Earl was being paid $130,000 plus benefits. Soon after his retirement he stood to make millions in a state-of-that-art contract with the General which restrained him from consultancy with any of the corporation's rivals. Despite his wealth and his influence, Earl considered himself a 'garden variety American'. He described his daily habits in an epic interview with the *Saturday Evening Post*, published in 1954. After his morning cold shower he liked to shave for perhaps half an hour. It took him maybe as long to select one of his hundred thousand or so suits. Of personal preferences he said, 'I remember faces and forget names. . . . When I hit a golf ball I am sorry to say it does not always stay on the fairway, and I have seen mallards fly off in excellent health after I have fired both barrels right at them. . . . I don't like to write letters. I like baseball and I love automobiles.'

General Motors announced his retirement on 1 December 1959 after thirty-two years during which his 'wizardry at creating eye appeal' had made him the leader of American automotive styling and made the American automotive industry the most powerful consumer force known before or since. As his mentor Alfred Sloan wrote, 'My generation had an opportunity unique in the history of American industry.' When they had all started in business the automobile was but a novelty. By the time they had finished it had become a symbol of American civilization.

These had been the years of optimism in Detroit. As if the unique opportunity to mould all the General's products, which included fridges, trains, exhibitions and appliances as well as cars, had not been enough, Harley Earl had had his own

LEFT Harley Earl rarely removed his tie at work, even in his own office. While still working for GM he formed his own design practice, Harley Earl Associates, in 1945, the General's only requirement being that he did not compete with the corporation.

LEFT One of Earl's major jobs as an independent was the interior design of the General Dynamics Convair 880, an unsuccessful competitor to the Boeing 707 and the Douglas DC-8.

design consultancy since 1945. Harley Earl Associates, which merged with Walter B. Ford Design Associates in 1964 to become Ford and Earl, was an operation which freed Harley to work beyond the very few aesthetic limitations which the General imposed on its most famous employee. The corporation's only stipulation was that Earl should not design products in direct competition with any elements of General Motors' own product line, so he concentrated on carpet-sweepers, aeroplane interiors, plumbers' showrooms, earth-movers and biscuits.

His passion for planes was not exorcized entirely by his adapting aeronautical motifs for his cars. He had been on the inaugural flight of Eastern Airlines' first Boeing 707, when, with veteran flyer Jimmy Doolittle at the controls, the first important jet had soared and whistled from Los Angeles to Seattle, and he had the chance to design the overhead passenger service modules for General Dynamics' failed rival to the 707, the Convair 880. He also designed the interior for the corporate Douglas DC-3 operated by Alcoa, the Aluminum Company of America. In fact, in his private capacity he was Alcoa's chief design consultant.

For both planes he released a pent-up explosion of formal and chromatic invention. Astonished Alcoa executives sat in Burns Aero seats upholstered in yellow Trilok, while their in-flight lounge chairs were of the same material but colliding in red. The Convair passengers sat on vacuum-formed foam shells covered in a fabric called Boltaron, alternating in 'morning and evening' sky blue, row by row. Matching throw cushions were upholstered in nylon fabric interwoven with gold Mylar. To alleviate the tunnelled-in claustrophobic impression which the long tube of the big jet's fuselage gave, Earl interrupted every fifth row of seats with a dropped ceiling section. The carpet he chose for in-flight purposes was a bright scarlet mohair; the ceiling and side walls were white with a gold-flecked

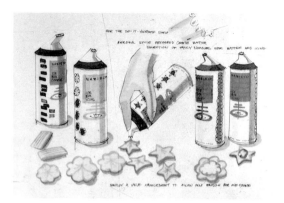

Nabisco, the cereal and cookie manufacturer, hired Earl as a consultant. When his team arrived at Nabisco's factories, they found the products wanting in consumer appeal and in semantics. The design solution was to make the form of the cookies more attractive, using shape and texture more effectively, and to propose supplying uncooked batter in aerosol cans so that the cook might express his or her own ideas of form.

and gold-spangled fabric; the bulkheads were striped. The Convair bombed.

Earl's other freelance jobs included a plumber's showroom in Warren, near the General's Tech Center and near his own adjacent offices. Here, as if in some act of ritual desecration, he ordered furniture by Charles Eames covered not in European matt black leather but in American orange Naugahyde. He also moved the Bissell carpet-sweeper company into the age of the Convair by designing for them a snappy logo and bringing the shell of their machine into the late 1950s by giving it jet plane details and radii. His most celebrated freelance job, however, was with biscuits.

Nabisco discovered design some time around 1959 when they invited Raymond Loewy to reshape their logotype. Fred Otaks, the company's vice president in charge of operations, had heard about Earl from reading in a newspaper how he had managed to make the mundane Bissell carpet-sweeper interesting. Otaks figured that if a carpet-sweeper could be interesting, then cookies could be equally fascinating, so he promptly commissioned Harley Earl to see what imagination could do to a standard commodity. Besides looking at the product, the cookie itself, Earl was also instructed to look at brand recognition, visual appeal and, for once, the ergonomics of the boxes.

The problem with Nabisco's cookies was that they were simply round, square or hexagonal. They had no *meaning*, and Earl had taught the American public via his cars that any product had to be more than merely an end in itself. Just as the car had to cease to be a development of the horseless carriage and the rural buggy, the cookie had to evolve from the simple state of the shape dictated by the 'mechanic who cut the first roller'. No-one had laboured over the Fig Newton as Harley Earl had laboured over the Cadillac Eldorado Seville Brougham.

Other Harley Earl designs as an independent included before and after presentations for Ban Roll-on Deodorant.

The Earl staff, perhaps in deference to its training at General Motors, were to let no restrictions cloud the imagination. They were only given a very quick tour of the factory, just in case learning too much about the realities of the manufacturing process would constrain the leaps of their imaginations. They were to *catch the mood* of how biscuits were made, but they were not to capture anything else. They had a look at the product and, isolating Peanut Cream Patties, they found that there was a problem with product identity. All the cookies looked much the same. 'They have a moulded look like untempered Masonite. A colour like wood or moulded phenolic. A texture as uninteresting as cardboard or craft paper. In short – they are completely devoid of the home-made look.'

The solution recommended by Harley Earl to Nabisco was exactly the same as the solution he had evolved thirty years before when he worked in General Motors Art and Colour Section: the company must exploit specialized tastes and dreams. Varieties of tastes and textures should be introduced: if the mass class market wanted handcrafted cookies, or apparently handcrafted cookies, then it must have them. The biscuit barrel was seen as an escape from the repetitive necessities of mass production, even though under Harley Earl's policy of multiplicity this had been a liberal enough regime. If the public wanted participation in its cookie consumption, then Harley Earl wanted to give that public aerosols filled with uncooked batter so that novel shapes and forms could be invented on the baking tray. What was more, ergonomics was to play a part in the cookie of the future. It was that moment in American social life when the cocktail dip, guacamole and cheese with chives, was being introduced and for this practice Harley Earl suggested that mechanically sound biscuits be wrought, the better to excavate these dips. He actually said that 'dips and spreads . . . have opened a new demand for well engineered and useful crackers'. However, unlike the General, the cookie manufacturers did not listen to his instructions. Earl's culinary inventions were never implemented directly, although Nabisco did inaugurate a New Products department, rather similar in concept to Art and Colour, as soon as they had read Earl's proposals.

Harley Earl's career was one of the most remarkable of any designer. His influence far outshone even Eliot Noyes' at IBM, although in retrospect both careers look like brief phenomena. He died in 1969, and the *New York Times* crisply declared in his obituary:

> In the mid 1930s he rubbed his thumbs across a sketch of a proposed new model, and erased the exterior running board from the American scene. He was credited with designing the first built-in luggage compartment to replace the bolted-on trunk; with the removal of the outside spare tire; with the two-tone paint job and the hardtop design.

Through imagination and the hard sell, Harley Earl clawed his way back along the production line to the point where, as a designer, he was able to influence every aspect of the character, formation and details of a General Motors' product. His sense of power and his own discovery of the seductive commercial force of novelty made him continuously discontent. Here, as in so many other aspects of his career, we can find in Harley Earl the elements of a larger metaphor about the American character during the country's most prosperous age.

Harley Earl *was* the American car and now that both have passed, the elegiac quality is all the more perceptible. In his book *The American People*, the English cultural anthropologist Geoffrey Gorer tried to determine the exact reasons why the Americans had an invincible taste for novelty, to accompany their established preference for rejecting authority. He determined that there was a direct connection between this phenomenon and the fact that while the first generation of immigrants had rejected their European homelands, the second generation, in a country without apparent frontiers, had rejected its own parents. In turn, the very size of the country required a commitment to mobility and this commitment was given expression in the American car.

In a sense, cars were the chief symbol of both the American dream and the American tragedy. The critic Eric Larrabee wrote:

> Stand at night, on a corner in a strange town, and watch the cars go by. What is there so poignant in this? A sense of private destinies, of each making his own choice, of being independent of everything but statistics. The car owners choose—or think they do—when to stop and start, where to go. The automobile offers a vista of escape: for the adolescent, from parental planning; for the Negro, from Jim Crow; and for others, from less formal restrictions on their freedom of movement. Thus they are liberated to the loneliness (and perplexity) of their independence, and thus travel on the highway at night acquires its own tones of adventure and sorrow.

So the car contained its own triumph and its own agony, but in its formation Harley Earl's contribution was an optimistic one: he subscribed to the pleasure principle. Now that we know there is nothing in the world as boring as a flush door, it is easier even than it was in the fifties to be moved by that faith in the magic of machines which allowed Harley Earl to say, 'You can design a car so that every time you get in it, it's a relief—you have a little vacation for a while.'

AFTERWORD

DESIGN IN AMERICA

THE FOUNDERS OF THE GENERAL MOTORS CORPORATION had sensed a great opportunity to organize manufacturing during America's first industrial revolution. The twin objectives of profits and growth were never questioned. William C. Durant, Sloan and Charles F. Kettering were never squeamish about their objectives: their finely tuned senses responded to the beauty of profits. Sloan, in his way, even defined the role of profits in a modern business: 'It is not a matter of the amount of profit but of the relation of that profit to the real worth of invested capital.'

Very familiar today, these perceptions were at the time like the definition of the Periodic Table of the elements. The fiscal procedures were primal. When Durant wanted to buy the Guardian Frigerator Company for the General's portfolio, he wrote his own cheque and the corporation repaid him about a year later. These people had the chance to be self-taught in business and very self-taught in very big business.

Alfred Sloan was the most remarkable of these businessmen. He turned round an all but bankrupt bearing manufacturer, the Hyatt Roller Bearing Company, on an investment of $5000, and in so doing learnt every aspect of the motor industry, from shop floor machine-minding to stock transfers. The worst sensation he ever experienced was growing pains. When W. C. Durant, fresh from his refrigerator acquisition, made an offer for the company, Sloan saw it with deliberation as another great opportunity to 'convert Hyatt's profits into readily saleable assets'. He got thirteen and a half million dollars, a portion of which came in the General's stock, and thus, moving from $5000 to many millions in a few ragtime years, he

LEFT Mr Corporation meets Mr Design: Alfred P. Sloan and Harley Earl shake hands in December 1958 at the dedication ceremony for Sloan's portrait in the GM Styling lobby.

assumed an 'important position' in what was to become America's major industrial undertaking.

It took a while for these founders of the American automobile industry to discover design. At first the word to them meant only the matter-of-fact solution to mechanical engineering problems or the ironing out of difficulties in the production process. With the urge to create volume, design meant the perfecting of manufacturing processes. Soon, however, they discovered a form of beauty separate from but related to the fascinating quest for profits. When they were persuaded for the first time that appearance might have an influence on sales, they did not call this perceptual innovation design; instead they called it *styling*. It was for them a real entity, another innovation in an evolving industry and one which took its place behind financial controls, centralized buying and the other procedural techniques which were the lore of a huge corporation.

They did not know that styling was to become a word of derision amongst Europeans, working in industries with smaller volumes in smaller markets. In the great reorganization of the industry during the twenties the General got itself into a position where it could supply a car for every individual consumer's needs. The General was learning to become more sophisticated. Unlike the first years of incorporation, when rival products from different divisions all took sales off each other, the General was smart and used styling as a business tool which interpreted with minute degrees of differentiation each level of the product line for each level of consumer. With an awe-inspiring respect for symmetry and for the market, during its prosperous years the General's stylists interpreted the customer's psyche and then fed it back to him in the form of chromium-plated, cart-sprung, barge-like, wraparound, tail-finned swank tanks. Orchestrating this razzle-dazzle made Harley Earl into a vice president, the first designer to assume that rank within a major American industry. He was an entertainer: he did not set out to be a world improver, but he was.

It is easy enough now to laugh at the business of gussying-up divisional body architecture into dreams measurable in dollars, but it is just as easy to lose sight of the purity of vision and the humanity that made it possible. And the un-complicated simplicity of it all. When Harley Earl used a word like 'streamline', no matter how many syllables he got into it he knew that it was a commodity which meant the odd Joe on the street had his life as a consumer enhanced. Never mind that Earl's phallic jelly-moulds did not conform to the European concept of what a 'streamlined, functional product' should be, Earl had the figures to back up his hunch. Anyway, Alfred Sloan had insisted that it could only ever be a cosmetic exercise, one that was 'definitely limited to the question of styling'.

In America there has always been a consumerist attitude to what Europeans have pettishly regarded as high art. The agonized concern to redefine social and moral principles in architecture was dubbed by two Americans the 'International Style'. When Earl wrote that the 1948 Cadillacs 'still bore a striking similarity to the plane's tail structure' he was not being silly, he was revealing a catholic interest in motif and meaning which had been lost in the empyrean of high-flown European debate about the nature and purpose of modern design.

The search for volume by a pursuit of the consumer's dreams made Earl permanently discontent. He could never feel secure when his attention was locked on to dreams which always had to face a public audit. When he had wrung the last drop of commercially measurable symbolism out of the imagery of the Lockheed P38, America entered the missile age and, the Americans being in Harley Earl's

1960 CHEVROLET CORVAIR

The 1960 Chevrolet Corvair was the first car produced wholly under the supervision of Earl's successor, William Mitchell. It was a clean, European-looking car with an ambitious engineering specification, featuring a rear-mounted flat-six engine and independent suspension, and was designed to offer a domestic product more sophisticated than the imported Volkswagens and Renaults. Although it was admired by the design profession, it was the car that crashed in 1961, provoking the consumer-campaigning attorney, Ralph Nader (RIGHT), to write his book *Unsafe at Any Speed*. Although the Supreme Court found in favour of GM, the damage had been done: the age of aggressive imagination in American car design was over.

OVERLEAF General Motors
staff party, *c.* 1957. Earl's
fascination with aerospace
extended even to his party
hats. On Earl's left is
William Mitchell, his
successor.

interpretation a people of motion, all car design circa 1957 was expected to anticipate the public's excitement with rocket-powered ballistics.

Yet there was a flaw in the system. Pledged to the pursuit of lowness and length, Earl began to realize just before 1960 that cars were reaching the maximum degree of lowness consistent with human beings of average agility being able to get in and out through the doors. But though cars had been stretched almost to the horizontal limits, Earl's innovation of styling for the annual model change meant the public expected a new shape every year.

Harley Earl did not see the trap. Close to his retirement he wrote:

Of two things I am sure. First, there will be continual changes which will make cars of the future ever more desirable. Secondly, these changes will match and in some cases set the pattern for the accelerating pace of American life. More and more they will be suggested by the customer himself. Beyond this, I'd rather try crossing a river on a path of bobbing soap cakes than make predictions about your car of tomorrow. The footing would be far safer!

Changes *were* about to be suggested by the customer himself, but they were changes of which Earl could never have dreamt. Less than three years after Harley Earl's retirement his dream car had become a public nightmare. Imaginative flair was replaced by self-parody in design, confidence was replaced by doubt and a desire to please the consumer's fantasies was replaced by the cynical marketing of tired products. The great age of American design did not outlive the man who created automotive style, Harley J. Earl, 1893–1969.

It is extraordinary that so little has been written about Harley Earl, America's most influential designer. No doubt there will be later studies which will locate Earl more precisely in history and culture than this necessarily loose first shot, but for the time being this is the fullest account there is of the life and work of the man who shaped the most familiar symbols of America: its cars.

This book owes its origins and its substance to a number of people who deserve to be mentioned, even if they would each not necessarily care to take responsibility for the appearance and character of the book. First is Lora Reidel of New York, a distant relative and New Yorker who knew Earl well. It was Mrs Riedel who sent over to England Frigidaires the size of catafalques and made Vauxhall cars available to immediate family at a discount price. These things brought me into my first contact with the material world of Harley Earl when I sensed the aroma of the American dream. Second to be mentioned is Mark Boxer, who had the idea to do the book in the first place, and third is that group of people who unselfishly gave their anecdotes and their advice: Michael Lamm of Stockton, California; James Earl of Durango, Colorado; Dick Teague of AMC, Detroit; Charles Jordan and Biljana Delevich of the General Motors Technical Center, Warren, Michigan, and Anatole Lapine of Porsche AG, Weissach, Germany. They all contributed to the book as much as I.

Meanwhile, Philip Castle's fine paintings have done more to evoke the memory of Harley Earl's achievement than all of us put together. . . .

SB

The author and publishers would like to thank the individuals and organizations mentioned below who kindly supplied the illustrations which appear on the following pages, and by whose permission they are reproduced:
Philip Castle: 2–3, 6, 7, 10–11, 14–15, 62
Ford & Earl Design Associates: 8, 53, 110, 112, 113, 114
General Motors: 1, 18, 20 below, 21, 24, 40, 48, 49, 51, 52, 54, 56, 57, 64, 68, 72, 76, 77, 80, 81, 82, 84, 85, 88, 100, 101, 107 below, 109, 118

Alan Irvine: 58, 59
Michael Lamm (courtesy of Art Earl): 20 above, 22, 23
National Motor Museum, Beaulieu: 26, 28, 30, 34, 41, 46, 50, 61, 92, 96, 105, 106, 107 above
Orbis Publishing Ltd (Photos by Laurie Caddell for Chrome: Glamour Cars of the Fifties by Brian Laban): 71, 91, 94, 98
Radio Times Hulton Picture Library: 122 below
Wolf Suschitzky: 126
Nicky Wright: 63, 66, 67, 86, 90, 95, 102

Numbers in *italics* refer to
illustrations

128